101 Affirmations for **Radical** *Self-Love*

Ann Thomas, Esq., CPCC

Copyright © 2011 Ann Thomas

All rights reserved.

ISBN: 1460976304
ISBN-13: 978-1460976302

DEDICATION

This book is dedicated to all the women who struggle to love themselves and long to be happy. You are loved, appreciated, and you are not alone! May this book be a gateway to your unyielding, radical to-the-core self-love. Know that you are, and always will be, more than enough!

CONTENTS

1 Affirmations for Your Spirit 1

2 Affirmations for Your Body & Sexuality 31

3 Affirmations for Your Emotions 51

4 Affirmations for Your Mind 81

ACKNOWLEDGMENTS

My first thanks and praise goes to the Divine. Without Spirit, I would not have been able to survive my personal trials and tribulations or write this book. I am so grateful and humbled!

I'd like to acknowledge and give thanks to my amazing wife, Nadine Roper. Without her unconditional love, support, and belief in me, I would not have had the courage to pursue my dreams of being a life coach and an author. She has been one of my biggest inspirations and a role model of self-love. Thank you, honey, for dedicating your time and love into editing this book and letting me endlessly run things by you.

I am grateful for my parents, Thomas Uthup and Mary Thomas. Despite how strained our relationship is, I love you infinitely and am grateful for the foundation you have provided me. Thank you for providing me with countless opportunities for me to grow and strengthen my spirit.

I am so grateful for my sister and best friend, Dr. Zinat Maniky, who was able to love me even when I couldn't love myself. Thank you for always believing in me and holding me in the highest light and love.

To all of the amazing people who have loved, supported, believed, and challenged me over the years, especially Lenese Herbert, Patricia Long, and Becky Boyd. Also, special thanks to Donniee Barnes for editing and giving me feedback on this book. I am deeply grateful to each of you for your love and support!

Finally, to my adorable puppy, Marco, who constantly teaches me unconditional love, patience, and how to be present.

INTRODUCTION

Welcome! *101 Affirmations for Radical Self-Love* was a labor of love. It is a compilation of the lessons I have learned over the last 16 years, as a part of my own personal and spiritual evolution. These are the very tools I have used to help me go from a woman who unconsciously (and sometimes overtly) hated herself to one who genuinely loves herself. May this book help you deepen your love for yourself and prevent you from engaging in thoughts and behaviors that sabotage you.

As the title suggests, there are 101 affirmations in this book, which are divided into four themes: affirmations for your spirit, body and sexuality, emotions, and mind. Each page offers you some insights and reflections on a particular topic as it relates to loving yourself more deeply. At the end of the commentary is an affirmation. I strongly recommend that you contemplate the messages, and when you are ready to read your affirmation, do so out loud.

Please note, I use the term God, Divine, Universe, Soul and Spirit interchangeably. What I mean by these terms is a spiritual source that serves as a higher power. Use whatever term resonates best with you – whether the terms are present in this book or not.

There are a number of ways to use this book. You can use it intuitively, asking your higher power to guide you to the right message, and then let your intuition take you to the right page. Or, you can simply choose to leaf through the book from front to back. Alternatively, you can focus on a particular section at a time.

With respect to the affirmations themselves, either pick a different one daily (or as you need it) or stick with the same message until you have truly internalized it. *Do not rush through this book.* It's not intended to be read like a novel. It requires contemplation and quiet reflection. However you choose to use this book, the most important thing is that you trust your gut. Use it in whatever way works best for you.

Even if we've never met, know that I love you. I believe in you. I appreciate you. And, I'm rooting for you to finally rid yourself of whatever it is that prevents you from being happy and loving yourself. When you love yourself, you can't help but make a positive impact on this world.

If you want more support in your journey to radical self-love, then email me at Ann@EvolvingGoddess.com or visit our website www.EvolvingGoddess.com to learn about our upcoming events and to receive a FREE copy of *Surviving the Dip: 10 Steps to Bounce Back Better Than Ever After Rejection.* As a bonus, you'll be automatically signed up for our weekly newsletter.

Remember, fall in love with yourself and your life *will* fall into place!

With love and gratitude from one evolving goddess to another,

Ann

AFFIRMATIONS FOR YOUR
Spirit

1. YOU ARE ONE WITH GOD

Many of us have been taught that God is a man out in the sky. Well, that's not the whole picture. Yes, the Divine is out in the sky . . . and in the trees, the birds, your mailperson, grocery clerk, and your spouse. The Divine is everywhere. Including within YOU!

You are a sacred spiritual being who is having a human experience. Do you get what that means? It means that you don't have to focus on the frailties you experience in life; you can trust that all is well in your world because you are, in fact, so much more than what you see. It means you are part of the One who has created everything; therefore you have access to the same creativity, love, and intelligence as the Divine.

How does it feel to know that you are God -- you and God are the same? Does it scare you? Does it stop you from harboring excuses for a poorly-lived life? Does it excite you? Do you see the infinite possibilities that can happen once you embrace this as your reality?

You are practicing radical self-love when you stop believing the lie that you are separate from the Divine. Radical self-love means that you know and accept that you are one with God. And, you accept all of the responsibilities that go with such knowledge.

I am one with the Divine. All things are possible for me and through me.

2. You are More Powerful Than You Realize

Marianne Williamson wrote, "Our deepest fear is not that we are inadequate. Our deepest fear is that we are powerful beyond measure." Yet, so many of us act as if we are truly powerless. Why? Because, somewhere along the way, we have been told outright and subtlely that our power is too much. Our laughter is too much. Our tears are too much. We have been taught by others that if we are to fit in, we must get with the program. So, we learned how to contain our power. We learned to mute it. We began the process of forgetting who we truly are.

Your powerlessness is an illusion! You are a spiritual being. You are one with the Divine. As a result, you can co-create the life that you want. Isn't that powerful?

Imagine if you could set an intention of what you want and, like a seed, it grows. Well, you can! There is nothing you can't do if you set your mind to it. Once you set your intention, get in touch with the feelings you would have if you actually obtained your heart's desires. Then, take consistent action. Like a farmer, you have to persistently pull out weeds (i.e., negative thinking and self-sabotaging behaviors), and nourish the seed by infusing yourself with positivity. Trust that the Divine will do its part. A farmer is not digging up the earth every five minutes to make sure that the seed grows. Instead, the farmer trusts that the Divine will do its part so long as the farmer does her part.

You are practicing radical self-love when you are steadfast and take action in the direction of your dreams while trusting that the Divine is doing its part. You can do anything. You can be anything. After all, you are powerful beyond measure!

I accept my power and I step into it fully.

3. THERE IS A PROMISE IN YOUR HEART

There is a promise in your heart. It reveals to you what your life's purpose is. A life purpose is not just about a career choice. It's about BEING on purpose – making conscious choices that really vibe with the core of you.

When you are consciously aware of your life purpose, you will step more fully into it. And your Soul will guide you in the direction of this purpose. You will know when you are living on purpose because you will *feel* it. Things will resonate. There is an ease and flow to your life. You feel at peace and joyous.

Contrarily, when you are living off purpose, you will feel "off." There will be a restlessness within you. You'll have a deep knowing that something is not quite right -- even if it appears to look alright on the surface.

When you sense the restlessness, it's time to pause and reflect. Think about a time in your life when everything felt perfect. What were you doing at that time? Who were you with? What made you feel joyful? How were you making use of your gifts and talents?

Now reflect on qualities, characteristics, and situations that you admire. How can you have more of that in your life?

By taking the time to answer these questions, you will begin to discover what your purpose is. When you do, it becomes a testament to the Universe that you accept and embrace your life purpose.

You are practicing radical self-love when you become consciously aware of your life purpose and take actions that resonate with that purpose.

I am living my purpose. I am living my truth!

4. Cultivate Your Intuition

We all have intuition. Essentially, it is our Spirit talking to us from a place of deeper knowing. Since we are one with the Divine, we are one with all things. It is through this interconnectivity that our Spirit is able to inform us of things from a place of knowing.

Although you are intuitive, there are things you can do to further develop it. First of all, start paying attention to the small quiet voice within you. That is the Divine trying to speak to you. In order to tune your station to WGOD FM, you need to be silent. You don't have to go into a full meditative practice (although meditation does help), but you do need to get quiet enough to begin to hear the voice of God talking to you.

Next, start practicing. Before you pick up a phone call, see if you can sense who is calling you. See if you can sense what is in the mail before you look at it. Begin to practice cultivating your intuition by actively trying to access it through these exercises.

Ask the Divine to help you hear and access your intuition better. There is a real power in asking for what you want. It gives a clear signal to the Universe. When you ask, you will receive.

You are practicing radical self-love when you learn to harness your intuition. It shows that you trust yourself and your Spirit. It demonstrates a willingness to remember that you are one with the Divine.

I connect to the universal knowing through my intuition.

5. Ask and You Shall Receive

There is a universal law that states that if you ask, you shall receive. We may know what we want, but many of us stop short of actually asking for it. Why? Because we don't feel deserving ("I feel guilty asking for help"). Or, because we feel as if we shouldn't have to ask ("I shouldn't have to ask my partner to be romantic"). Or, you simply don't want to ask ("I don't want to ask my boss for a raise").

Instead of asking, we brood. We create a state of unfulfillment and emotional chaos because we are longing for something, yet, we are not able to receive it. No matter how difficult it may be to ask, you must ask if you want to receive.

From a spiritual perspective, when you ask someone for something, you are engaging in two spiritual principles. The first spiritual principle relates to giving. You are giving a gift to the other person when you trust in their ability to give you what you have asked for. You are also blessing them with an opportunity to gift you, which in turn, opens up blessings for them.

The second spiritual principle you evoke is that of receiving. Receiving is equally as important as giving because it allows balance. When you are always giving and don't allow yourself to receive, you are creating an imbalance. This imbalance is not without consequence. Think about the last time you felt like you've given too much. What happened? Didn't you end up feeling resentful and tired?

You are practicing radical self-love when you assert your right to ask for what you want and are open to receiving it.

I honor myself by exercising my right to ask for what I want. I am open to receiving what I ask for or something better.

6. You are Connected to Divine Intelligence

Have you ever doubted your intelligence? Have you ever thought that you are not smart (or smart enough)? If so, you were believing a lie.

You are made of the same substance as the Divine, as Einstein, and as the people you look up to and admire. When you start to have doubts about your intelligence, remind yourself that you are one with Divine Intelligence.

When in doubt, ask the Divine to show you what you need to know. Ask that it be revealed to you vividly and clearly. Ask to have your connection to Divine Intelligence strengthened and you will receive it.

If you ask and you are not receiving, you may be blocked. Typically, the block is the result of you believing that you are separate from the Divine. You are holding limiting beliefs about yourself and what you are capable of.

To remove this block, do the following exercise:

> Close your eyes and take a deep breath. Imagine that there is a brilliant light that encompasses the sky. It is the light of the Divine. This light surrounds you. It envelopes you in its warmth. This light holds an infinite intelligence.
>
> Now, imagine that the light of the Divine pours into you through a small opening at the top of your head. This light fills you, starting from the top of your head, down your face, through your neck and shoulders, flowing to your heart center, moving steadily down to your solar plexus, across your hips, and down your legs; finally, it connects with the Earth through the soles of your feet. This Divine light now flows steadily around you and through you. All that

you need to know is now present and available to you. Now, take a moment to ask the Divine what you are longing to know. Listen for the answer.

You are practicing radical self-love when you remember that you are connected to Divine Intelligence and all that you need to know is revealed to you at exactly the right moment.

I am one with the Divine; therefore, I have access to infinite intelligence. I now choose to access more of this divine, universal intelligence that flows around me, in me, and through me. I am brilliant!

7. Forgive Yourself

Yes, you have let yourself down. Maybe you let yourself go. Maybe you stayed in a relationship that wasn't working longer than you should have. Perhaps you keep breaking the promises that you make to yourself. You have been carrying this disappointment and disgust with you for long enough. It's time to lay your burdens down.

The resentments you have toward yourself are toxic. Like all things in this Universe, like attracts like. So too, the toxic thoughts and feelings that are generated by your resentments toward yourself are attracting more toxicity into your life. For example, let's say you gained an extra 15 pounds. Instead of forgiving yourself, you beat yourself up. In doing you so, you can't combat the negative, lethargic energy that created the weight gain in the first place. Instead, you add a new layer of negativity into your experience, and that, too, will manifest on your physical form.

To experience radical self-love you must forgive yourself. Forgive yourself for each and every situation where you betrayed yourself, caused yourself harm, and failed to stand up for yourself. Forgive yourself for anything and everything that you continue to hold against yourself. Let it go. Release it and let there be room for better things.

I forgive myself, understanding with love and compassion that I did the best that I could with what I knew at the time. I release all resentments I hold against myself. I am free!

8. PRACTICE SEVA

"Seva" is a Sanskrit word that means selfless service. It is a way in which we get to honor the Divine in ourselves and others.

You may be wondering what selfless service has to do with radical self-love. When you give to another in selfless service, you are simultaneously opening up the opportunity to receive more. Through your giving, you show the Universe that you use your gifts and talents to promote abundance in this world.

When you are stingy, the Universe will be stingy with you. When you are generous, the Universe will be generous with you!

When you give to another in selfless service, you will receive certain incidental benefits. You will feel good about helping another. You will feel gratitude for what you have and for your ability to give. You are activating the Divine in you.

The Divine is very generous. It continues to create things that affirm life. It provides us with beautiful things to look at. It gives to us from a place of love. Allow yourself to align more closely with the Divine by giving in selfless service.

You are practicing radical self-love and stepping more fully into your Divine essence when you offer your time and your gifts in selfless service to others.

I am abundant! I choose to give because I have so much to give. As an act of my divine nature, I release my love and generosity, which, in turn, returns to me multiplied.

9. What You See In Others Is Already Within You

Have you ever admired someone and wished that you had what they had? Maybe you admire their leadership qualities or how organized they are. Perhaps it's how well they relate to others or how spiritual and grounded they seem. Whatever it may be, when you are able to notice something in another that really *resonates* with you, you are tapping into something that is already within you. It may not be activated in the same way or to the same degree as what you saw in the other person, but it does exist in you.

The beauty about recognizing that the qualities you admire in another exist in you is that it becomes easier to cultivate and grow those qualities. It's like trying to ignite a fire and being fortunate enough to have lit embers under the ash. You are not starting from scratch!

However, the flip side is also true. Just like qualities you admire are reflections of you, so too, are qualities that you dislike. For example, if you feel like your partner is emotionally unavailable, chances are you are too. Ask yourself, "Where am I being emotionally unavailable?" Perhaps you are being emotionally unavailable to yourself by placing too much attention on the relationship. Or, your neediness may cause you to be unavailable to your partner.

You are practicing radical self-love when you realize that the qualities you recognize in another – both, what you like and dislike – serve as a mirror, reflecting what is going on within you.

What I see in others is a reflection of that which is already within me. I am loving and compassionate with what I see in myself and in others. I choose wisely the qualities I want to cultivate and those that I want to mitigate.

10. Cultivate A Strong Foundation

When it comes to buildings, many of us know that in order for the structure to last, it has to have a strong foundation. You wouldn't want to build a house on quicksand! Well, the same concept applies to having a happy, fulfilling life. In order to be happy *consistently*, you have to ensure that your foundation is strong.

One aspect of a strong foundation is having a strong connection to your Soul. It's about realizing that you are far more than just the sum of your experiences. You are not just a woman. You are a goddess – an infinite, divine being!

Just because you're a goddess, however, doesn't mean that you know it or always feel like it. In fact, most of us forget just how special we really are. We believe that something is wrong with us. We believe that we are not good enough. We believe our worth is tied to what we do, what people think of us, or our social status. Well, that's a lie! These statements are mere cracks in your foundation.

Developing a connection with your Soul helps you to remember the truth – that you really are so magnificent and beautiful, courageous and compassionate, loving and strong. In a word, perfect!

You are practicing radical self-love when you develop a conscious connection with your Soul and allow this to be the foundation of your life.

I am a magnificent divine goddess! My foundation is unshakeable. My foundation is the Divine itself!

11. Trust in Divine Timing

You're doing it. You set the intention for what you want. You're visualizing it. You have written a vision statement that is expressed in the present tense and specifically and clearly states what you want. You are taking consistent action in the direction of your dreams. *Yet, nothing is happening!* Don't get discouraged! It will happen. And, it will happen at exactly the right time. Divine time.

What often looks like a disappointment, a setback or an obstacle can be the Divine stepping in to ensure that the timing for when you receive what you want is perfect. Maybe you are being delayed because what you dream of isn't quite big enough since you are capable of so much more. Perhaps if you received it now, you would not be completely emotionally, mentally, and spiritually ready to receive it. As a result, you could squander your gift and the Divine finds it too important for you to squander. Therefore, it waits until the perfect time. Be patient. Trust that all that is happening is happening for *your* highest and greatest good.

You are practicing radical self-love when you realize the Divine is on your side. When things don't happen on your timetable, trust that the Divine is working out the perfect time to give you what you are longing for. In the meantime, embrace the journey because it is preparing you for receiving the gifts that you've asked for.

I trust in Divine timing and know that all that is in my best interest will occur exactly when and in the order that it must.

12. Give Up the Struggle

Sometimes we make our lives so much more complicated than it needs to be. We become addicted to the notion that things have to be hard in order for us to succeed. Give up the struggle!

When you find yourself struggling with something, surrender it to the Divine. Ask yourself, "What would make this easy?" Figure out what you might be doing to get in your own way. Is there a short cut that could help? Is there a person that could advise or coach you?

What would it be like if you surrendered your struggles to God? Have you associated a part of your identity with struggle and drama? If so, it's time to give it up.

Imagine what's possible without the struggle – how much more could you accomplish; how much happier could you be?

Frederick Douglass wrote, "If there is no struggle, there is no progress." It's a motto you could live by, but why would you? You can progress without being in the mindset of struggle. Yes, detours and setbacks will happen. You will be tested. That's a part of life. But, you don't have to struggle with it. You don't have to resist it. It is your resistance that creates struggle. That is what makes you view a setback or an obstacle as devastating. Instead of resisting the natural ebbs and flows of life, go with it. It's preparing you for your next expansion!

You are practicing radical self-love when you find ways to reduce the struggle in your life by ceasing your resistance to the natural ebbs and flows of life.

I surrender my struggles to the Divine and let go of my hidden resistance to a life without struggle. Whatever comes my way, I'll handle it. There is nothing I can't do with God as my co-creator!

13. Retreat

Sometimes you just need to check out from your day-to-day responsibilities. You need to take a real break. You need a retreat.

A retreat is a time to unplug from this physical plane and get in touch with that which feeds you. There is so much going on in our worlds – we have responsibilities at work, to our families, to our significant others, our friends, and our pets. We are always on the go. Not even our vacations tend to be relaxing. That is why we, more than ever, need to completely unplug.

A retreat will help you reconnect with your source – the Divine within. It will rebalance you and prepare you for the next level of growth or responsibilities that lay before you.

Despite all the benefits of taking a retreat, you may be thinking, "I can't afford to take the time off. I have too much to do. I'll be so behind when I get back." Frankly, you can't afford *not* to! The time you take to retreat comes back to you multiplied – in energy, in a fresh perspective, and in peace. You have a stronger sense of who you are. You are better able to access your divinity – that place from which you get to create a life that is less stressful. A life that is abundant with ease and flow.

You are practicing radical self-love when you allow yourself to retreat from your everyday responsibilities and completely unplug. What you gain in peace, inner strength, and energy far outweighs any excuses you may have that prevent you from taking the time for self-care.

I love and honor myself by regularly taking time to retreat and rejuvenate, knowing that the time spent revitalizes my mind, body and soul.

14. THE TESTS OF LIFE

Sometimes, despite our best efforts to do the right thing and be a good person, we are faced with difficult situations. This is the time when we tend to get discouraged. Things feel hopeless. We want to give up.

Don't give up! This is the time to hunker down. This is the time to stay in faith. This is the time to trust the Divine. The Divine will not fail you! Everything is going to work out. You are merely being tested.

You've taken tests in school. Despite your anxiety or nervousness before the exam, what did you do during the test? You simply answered one question at a time. If you felt that a particular question was too difficult, you redirected your attention to another question that was easier to answer. When you were completely stumped, you made your best guess as to how to answer and moved on. And then, the time was up.

Apply these lessons from taking exams in school to the tests in your life. Know that your tests are time-limited. They will not go on forever. Trust in your preparation. Recall what you have studied – meaning the tools for a positive life. You can't complete a test in school by looking at the whole exam. You have to answer one question at a time. Likewise, stay focused on your very next step. Take one baby step at a time. Before long, your test will be up!

You are practicing radical self-love when you trust the Divine during the tests in your life. Apply the lessons you've learned in taking exams in school to the tests in your life. You have the ability to take the very next step.

I trust the Divine, knowing that my tests are time-limited and I always pass!

15. Cease Gossiping

Gossip is harmful. Words carry an energetic power. When you gossip about someone, you are putting negative energy out into the world. It also puts you out of integrity. You are in judgment of others.

When you gossip, you are operating at a lower vibration. Everything in this Universe operates on a certain vibrational frequency. Higher vibrational energies move faster, are lighter and are more positive. They include joy, abundance, and compassion. Lower vibrational energies are slower and dense, such as anger, sadness, and envy.

Only things that are a vibrational match can connect with one another. For example, think of a dog whistle. It cannot be heard by human ears because the sound is at a vibrational level inconsistent with ours. Because gossip is a lower vibration, those who gossip will attract things that also vibrate at a lower level. If you want to attract more positive things, you have to operate from a higher vibration.

When you cease to gossip about others, you will notice things begin to shift and open up for you. You will gain more time. You will attract less circumstances in your life by which others would gossip about you. You may also notice a shift in the people that you spend time with because you will be attracting people who engage in more positive and productive behaviors.

You are practicing radical self-love when you stop gossiping about others. Instead, focus on what you want in your life and see others with compassion and in the best possible light.

I choose to see the best in others. I use my words carefully and responsibly. I am a beacon of love and light!

16. Practice Gratitude

You have so very much to be grateful for! You are alive. You have a body that functions. You have a mind that allows you to read this. You get to breathe without having to think about it.

Each day there are a multitude of blessings that happen to you. It's important to start appreciating them. What you focus your attention on expands. Therefore, if you spend time each day in gratitude for what you have, you are going to naturally attract more things that make you feel grateful. Moreover, gratitude is a high vibrational energy. When you are feeling low, angry, sad or any other "downer" feeling, begin to notice some things that you are grateful for. It will help raise your overall mood and vibration.

Go ahead. Give God a shout out! Speak your gratefulness out loud. Or write it down. Thinking it is also good, but you are adding more oomph to your appreciation when you take the time to give it the additional energy that writing and speaking offer. To keep you in the spirit of appreciation, get a beautiful journal and dedicate it solely to things you are grateful for. Feel free to write in it before you go to sleep or anytime you feel inspired.

You are practicing radical self-love when you realize that there is *always* something to appreciate and be grateful for – even in the midst of your darkest days and hours.

I am so happy and grateful for all that I have and all that I am!

17. EXPERIENCE THE DIVINE

You can talk about God all you want. You can study different spiritual and religious texts. But, it is not until you become still and look within that you will truly *know* God.

Meditation is the highest form of prayer because it allows you to truly get connected with the Divine. When you are able to be still and look within, you will start to recognize the Divine in you. Meditation helps break the illusion of separation from God. It helps you to realize and remember that you are one with God.

Imagine really *knowing* that you are one with God. If you truly believed that, wouldn't your life be radically different than it is now? You would know that no matter what, it's all good. Everything that happens serves a higher purpose. You would know that you are always provided for and taken care of. You would be able to tap into the abundance in this world, simply because you know you have a right to it. You are part of all that exists, and all that exists is yours. It is all a part of your Queendom!

You are practicing radical self-love when you make the time to meditate, knowing that the stillness helps you to remember who you truly are – an incarnation of the Divine.

I embrace stillness. I am one with God.

18. Welcome Chaos

When you step up your game, expect chaos. Chaos is a normal part of any growth process. The Universe evolves through chaos. We see evidence of this through how the planets were formed. We see it with the birth of a new child. When a caterpillar is in its cocoon and transforming itself into a butterfly, the process is chaotic and even painful. But the most beautiful and amazing things emerge from that chaos.

Chaos serves two purposes. First, it is a test to see whether you truly want what you say you want. If at the first sign of things going wrong you abandon ship, then you are demonstrating to the Universe that you really don't want it. You're not ready. Yes, it's normal to want to run back to familiar territory. But if you do, then you will continue to see the same results.

Second, chaos serves as an opportunity to allow the things that have been deeply rooted in your subconscious to rise to the top so that they may be released. There are beliefs you hold that are rooted in your subconscious that have created the life and circumstances that you have lived until now. When you choose to step up your game, these beliefs don't automatically disappear. They rise from what is below your consciousness to the surface. It provides you with an opportunity to notice where you may need some additional healing, a change in thinking, or some other way of letting go what no longer serves you.

You are practicing radical self-love when you view the chaos in your life as a teaching opportunity.

Chaos is a natural stage of growth. I choose to learn from the chaos in my life. It reveals where I can deepen my self-love, expunge limiting beliefs, and heal.

19. Embrace Silence

In order to know the Divine within you, you must get quiet. It is often said that prayer is when we talk to God, and meditation is when God talks to us. It is in stillness, that we are able to truly "hear" the quiet voice that is within. This voice does not yell. It does not beg for your attention. Yet, it is always speaking to you. It is the feeling you get when you decide not to walk down a particular street. It is the gentle tug within you that talks you off of the ledge when you're struggling. It's the small thought that crosses your mind and tells you to call a friend only to find out that they were in need at that very moment.

You can learn to hear God's voice by developing a practice of meditation. Meditation is just a fancy word for getting silent, turning your attention inward. To help you tame what the Buddhists call "monkey mind," pick one object to focus your attention on. It could be your breath. It could be a candle. It could be a particular point on the wall. Whenever you notice your mind wandering, simply redirect your attention to that object.

As you focus your attention, listen. Don't just listen with your physical ears; listen with your Soul's ears. Listen from within. You may not hear anything at first. It's ok. Be patient. You will hear God speak to you. And the more you practice, the more often you'll hear it and the easier it gets to distinguish God's voice from the chatter of your monkey mind.

You are practicing radical self-love when you learn to embrace silence.

I welcome silence as a pathway to strengthen my connection to God.

20. The Universe Likes Consistency

If you want to grab the Universe's attention, be consistent. Be steadfast in what you desire. Consistency is confirmation that you want something to manifest quickly. Your being consistent is also a reaffirmation of your commitment. When you are truly committed to something, you will do whatever it takes, and pursue it persistently, to achieve it.

Being consistent doesn't mean that you have to have it all figured out. You don't. You simply have to be consistent in taking small action steps in the direction of your dreams.

Maybe you want to find a new job that you're passionate about. Maybe you want to improve your love life. Perhaps you want to lose weight or be better organized. Whatever it is that you want to accomplish, make the commitment to be consistent in your action steps. You cannot simply think your way to your goals. Your thoughts have to be coupled with action.

Small steps are all that's necessary. Spend a few minutes every day taking action on the things that you want. Get clear and stay focused to prevent self-sabotage. Don't give yourself more goals than you can handle at any one time. It will prevent you from being able to achieve any of it.

You are practicing radical self-love when you take consistent action toward your dreams. Whenever you're in doubt, ask your Spirit to just show you what your next immediate step should be. Then go do it!

I fully commit to achieving my dreams. Therefore, I spend a few minutes each day in action toward achieving them. My actions are a signal to the Universe of my deep desire and commitment!

21. Become a Warrior of Love

Love is pure. Love is boundary-less. Love is real. It is our essence. Love is Universal. It is more than the incredible feeling we have when we first fall in love with someone. It is an absolute unconditional acceptance.

We don't see too much love in our world. Today, we experience more of the absence of love than its presence. We see fear. We see anger. We see love being suppressed.

When you are in struggle, you are suppressing love. When you hide, you are suppressing love. When you withdraw, you are suppressing love. When you numb yourself, you are suppressing love.

Each time you feel the presence of love, know that it is reminder and an invitation. A reminder of who you truly are and an invitation to more fully reclaim this lost part of yourself.

Our world needs healing. You need healing. This healing happens only through love. And so, this is a call to action. Dare to become a warrior of love. Not a mean, vicious warrior, but a loving one. Warriors are steadfast, they stay focused on the goal, they are disciplined, and they keep moving despite setbacks. They take all these actions so that they can achieve freedom. Love is the ultimate freedom.

You are practicing radical self-love when you choose to become a warrior of love. Love yourself unconditionally. Love others. Forgive. Be forgiven. Be free.

I am a warrior of love. I accept my call to action to be a beacon of love and to bring more love to this world, starting with the love I have for myself!

22. TO THINE OWN SELF BE TRUE

You are a unique manifestation of the Divine. No one else walks your path. No one else knows what is within you. No one else has shared in all that encompasses you – your experiences, your thoughts, and your feelings. You are not cut out from a cookie cutter! You are like a snowflake – unique and exquisite. So, why would you try to be like anyone else?

To be true to your authentic self is the greatest expression of self-love and divine love. God made you exactly as you are. You are perfect exactly as you are. Your perfection may not look the same as your neighbors. So what? Do you really think that the Divine has a limited range of expression? Is the Divine only white or black or brown? Is it only male or female? Or is the Divine all encompassing? If it were all encompassing, wouldn't there be room for you to be exactly as you are? In fact, if you refused to be your authentic self, you are denying the Divine an opportunity to express itself through you. You don't need to be like Mary. Mary is here to be Mary. You need to be you!

Instead of suppressing your authentic self, express it. Let it shine! It is divine. The world needs YOU. Otherwise, you wouldn't be here. The world needs your thoughts, your words, your analysis, and your gifts. You are a unique and essential representation of the Divine. Nothing that is divine should be reduced to conformity.

You are practicing radical self-love when you realize that being true to your own self is a divinely-ordained expression of self-love that is necessary for this world.

I choose to always be true to myself because I am a unique expression of divine love!

23. Manifest Your Dream Life

The secret to creating a life that you are in love with is to have a vision of what you want, feel what it would be like to live that vision, and keep that vision at the forefront of your mind with great faith that it will come to fruition.

Faith is key. Have faith even when you don't *see* the results. There is a mystery to how things work. Not everything will be seen. There is a part of manifesting your desires that occurs in the spiritual realm – at a level where you would not be able to observe it. Don't just rely on your physical senses to inform you about whether your dreams are manifesting.

When you have a vision that you can clearly and specifically see and feel, it is as if you are placing an order to the Universe for that vision. However, when you entertain doubt, it's as if you go back and cancel your order. Instead of allowing doubt to enter the space when you don't see progress, hold faith. Surrender your doubt to Spirit. Let Spirit know that you noticed the doubt, and you are releasing it to Spirit to take it away. Then refocus and recommit to your vision. Specifically, reconnect not only with the visual aspect of your vision, but reconnect with how it would feel to *live* that vision.

You are practicing radical self-love when you hold your vision in faith while taking action toward it. When you do, its manifestation is inevitable.

What I envision is already manifested in Spirit and is in the process of physical manifestation. I lovingly await its arrival in faith and with joy!

24. Know Thyself

Despite the fact that you've been with yourself all your life, you may not necessarily know yourself. To know yourself, you have to take the time for self-reflection. You need to be willing to hear what others who are close to you perceive of you. You need to take the time to read and experience things that will help you grow and evolve. You need to apply what you have learned.

Don't be afraid to get to know yourself. Yes, you will discover some things you don't like about yourself. So what? Instead of lamenting about it and beating yourself up, make the decision to change what you don't like about yourself. It could be a personality quirk, something about your physical attributes, or it could be how you respond and react to things.

Believe me, although you'll find a few things you don't care for, there's so much more that is absolutely precious about you. You are amazing! You are as beautiful and as multi-faceted as a sunset. You are so interesting. There is so much to explore and learn. And once you begin this journey to deeper self-discovery, you are naturally going to attract better things in your life. You will step into the woman you truly are – the one you can see yourself becoming!

You are practicing radical self-love when you take the time to discover and truly know yourself. Through this process, you will learn to accept yourself without judgment, view your behaviors with compassion, and most importantly, love yourself unconditionally!

I am on a journey to learn everything there is to learn about me!

25. What You Notice Magnifies

Whatever you place your attention on expands. When you place your attention on an item, it is a signal to the Universe that it's something that you're interested in. So, the Universe gives you more of it. If you are used to focusing on what's wrong and what's not working, then you will continue to attract more experiences that don't work.

It's understandable that you will notice what's wrong and what's not working. Those are the types of things that tend to grab our attention. But now, you have an opportunity to grab hold of your attention. Redirect your attention to focus on your intentions.

What do you want in your life? Do you want to be thinner? Then stop focusing on the fat on your body or on others. Instead, envision yourself at your ideal weight and body. Do you long to be in a relationship? If so, then focus on your ideal mate. Look at images of couples in love and make room for a relationship. Do you want a change in your career? Then, focus on doing the best job you can now and on the specific characteristics of what you want. The key, however, is when you observe others who have what you are longing for, don't observe from a place of envy. Instead, observe from a place of admiration and trust that it's already yours waiting to manifest!

If you happen to focus on the negative, don't beat yourself up. Simply redirect your attention to what you want. Give yourself time to allow the laws of the Universe to work.

You are practicing radical self-love when you consciously focus your attention on your intentions.

I direct my thoughts and attention to what I want, trusting in the universal laws and knowing that what I want is already mine!

AFFIRMATIONS FOR YOUR

Body

&

Sexuality

26. Your Body is a Divine Temple

A temple is a place dedicated to the service or worship of one or more deities. The deity your body primarily serves is the goddess that resides within you. Simply put, you are a divine being. The Divine is not something that resides outside of you. You and the Divine are one. All that you seek from God, you can receive by going within.

How would you treat your body if you knew that God resides within it? Wouldn't you make sure that it was clean and properly cared for? Wouldn't you repair what is damaged? Most importantly, wouldn't you revere it?

How would you conduct yourself if you realized your body carried something precious inside? Have you ever seen the way a pregnant woman walks? She walks like she has a beautiful secret – she walks knowing that she carries something precious within her. YOU are that something precious! Your body has been gifted with the privilege of housing your sacred, divine essence. What a joy, honor and sacred duty!

You are practicing radical self-love when you accept that your body is a temple that houses the Divine.

My body is a temple that houses the Divine. I treat this temple with love, respect, and the utmost regard. I lovingly care for and give thanks to my body temple.

27. Your Body is Perfect

There is nothing wrong with your body. We women are so hard on ourselves and go around criticizing our bodies so much that we can't even see it as a whole unit. Instead, all we see are parts. We focus on our "fat thighs," "muffin top," zits and scars. All we see is what's wrong with us.

Your body is not a series of imperfections. It is an exquisite piece of art. Every angle, curve, color and texture has combined in a unique configuration to form you. And you are a masterpiece! After all, you are created by the Divine. Could you imagine someone telling Michael Angelo that the Mona Lisa was not a magnificent piece of art because one of his brush strokes was a bit thick? No! Yet, we do that to ourselves all the time.

Take a moment to stop and see the perfection that your body is. Think about how beautiful your curves and angles are. Notice the treasures that your body holds. Be mindful of the fact that your body works on your behalf 24 hours a day, every day. Your legs take you where you want to go, your heart beats, and your lungs continue to breathe even as you are in the deepest sleep. Your body is perfect.

You are practicing radical self-love when you refuse to only focus on what you think is imperfect about your body and develop a larger lens with which to see your body.

My body is perfect. I see it for all its glory and I am so grateful to have this brilliant masterpiece as my companion throughout this lifetime!

28. Go on a Treasure Hunt

We often spend so much time focusing on the things about our bodies that we don't like – our fat belly, our wrinkles, our big nose, our yellow teeth, our pimples. Despite these seeming imperfections, your body contains so many treasures! Go on a treasure hunt and find all of the treasures on your body.

Start from the bottom and work your way up. Take a look at your feet. What's pretty about them? Don't take "nothing" for an answer. Find *something* – even if it's a mole on your pinky toe – and celebrate it.

Repeat the exercise by examining your legs, hips, waist, chest, arms, hands, shoulders, neck, face and head. Don't forget to inspect every single inch of you. Your goal is to find a new treasure on every aspect of your body.

Look for unique things. Like how your skin looks in a certain light. Look at your body in segments, and then take a look at your body as a whole. What's something new and beautiful about your silhouette that you have never noticed before? Make it your business to find everything on your body that you find scintillating, beautiful, exotic, fun, and sensuous. Notice where your body curves, where it angles, and where it lay straight. Remember to celebrate each of your treasures.

You are practicing radical self-love when you pay attention to the treasures of your body, rather than focusing only on what you don't like or wish to improve.

My body is an island of treasures! I love and celebrate each one of them!

29. Eat Only for Nourishment

Too often, we eat to numb ourselves. We eat because we are depressed. We eat because we're bored. We eat because we are lonely. Well, these are not the reasons why we should eat. Food is a gift that is meant to be used to nourish your body. We all need a balance of different types of foods to give us energy.

You are not powerless over food! You absolutely can control what you eat, how much you eat, and when you eat. The first thing to do is notice what you are using the food for. What are you trying to soothe with the food? What feelings are you trying to suppress? No matter what it is, know that you are fully capable of handling it. No amount of fear, sadness, and loneliness will break you! In fact, avoiding the emotion makes it a bigger deal than it actually is. So go ahead and face the pain, loneliness, sadness, and anger. Welcome it with love and compassion. Let it come up fully so that it can leave you quickly. Resist the temptation to numb yourself with food.

From this moment forward, allow yourself to be fully present with your food. Take your food in with all five senses. Don't allow for distractions (like television) to get in the way. Simply be present to the sacred and privileged act of eating. And bear in mind what the true reason for eating is – to provide you with nourishment. To give you enough fuel to live each day to the fullest!

You are practicing radical self-love when you choose to eat only for nourishment and resist the temptation to use food to self-medicate or numb.

I love and accept myself. Therefore, I choose to eat only for the sake of nourishing my body and providing it with the fuel that it needs to help me live a fulfilling life.

30. Stop Shaming Your Body

Have you ever looked in the mirror and felt disgusted at what you saw? Have you ever looked at another woman and envied something about her appearance, wishing that you looked like that? Do you constantly berate a part of your body? If so, you are shaming your body.

We have to stop this abuse! It is absolutely abusive to shame our bodies. Our bodies are divine gifts. And even with the so-called deficiencies, it is a blessing. There are infinitely more good things about your body than flaws. For example, your organs work around the clock ensuring that you have air to breathe, your toxins are removed, and your systems are working. Your beautiful body is nothing short of magical!

When we were nothing but pure spirit form, we couldn't wait to get into a physical form. We couldn't wait to have these bodies so that we could feel emotions, experience things with our senses, and use our minds to create an ever-expansive, freer, and fuller version of ourselves. Now, many of us have forgotten how precious this gift really is.

Instead of shaming your body, practice gratitude for it. Practice gratitude for every cell, every hair, every pigment, and every freckle. Be grateful for your organs, your eyes, limbs, eyebrows, teeth, and gums. See yourself from the eyes of someone who adores you. You are beautiful. Own it!

You are practicing radical self-love when you remain conscious of how precious your body is, and notice how its magic and beauty far exceeds any flaws you may perceive.

My body is gorgeous and precious. I am grateful for my body, from my head to my toes, from my skin to my cells, from my organs to the blood that flows through me. I love and appreciate my beautiful body!

31. Pay Attention to Your Body Before It Breaks Down

We live in a very fast-paced world. We tend to keep going, and pushing ourselves. Even our days off from work are filled with things to do. And in the process of doing and living, many of us tend to ignore our bodies. We keep pushing it to do more. We don't rest.

Eventually, this pace catches up with us. We often don't pay attention to our bodies until it breaks down. We won't allow ourselves to rest until we get sick or injured and are forced to rest.

Our bodies provide us with a wealth of information about what is happening within our subconscious. When you manifest an illness or ailment, you most likely have an unresolved issue lingering in your subconscious. For example, when you have a boil or blister, it represents unresolved anger that is seeking to be released. To discover the mind-body connection between most common diseases, read *Heal Your Body* by Louise Hay.

Rest and recreation are essential to our wellbeing. If you don't allow yourself to stop, cocoon, and rejuvenate, you will burn out. Your body will force you to pay attention to it by making you sick.

You are practicing radical self-love when you pay attention to your body and give yourself time to rest. Recreation helps us to re-create ourselves. When you are sick, take the time to investigate any possible unresolved emotions or issues that may be the true reason for the illness.

I am conscious about the needs of my body. I deserve to rest and I give myself permission to rest and recreate. I deal with my emotions fully so that they do not seek release through disease or illness.

32. CREATE A DAILY DIGNITY RITUAL

Most of us start our days in a mad rush. We wake up, dash out of bed, jump in the shower and immediately start thinking about all the things we need to do, then we quickly grab a cup of coffee or tea and something to eat (if we're lucky) and rush to work. Think about the impact this morning routine has on your day. Are you less patient? Do you find it hard to concentrate? Do you feel exhausted? If so, create a daily dignity ritual and observe the impact it has on your life.

A daily dignity ritual is a ritual of self-care that you commit to doing each morning. The intent is to help you start your day right, grounded in yourself and your Spirit. The ritual can be as simple or as elaborate as you desire. But the key is to start the day with self-care.

If you are limited in time, incorporate a self-care ritual into what you already do. For example, appreciate your body while you shower or repeat your affirmations while getting dressed. When you have more time, create a more elaborate ritual such as lighting a candle and meditating or writing in your journal. There's no end to the creative things you can do to start the morning with loving self-care.

Having a daily dignity ritual has a number of benefits. It will center and ground you. You will feel loved and less emotionally needy because you are giving yourself the love that you seek. You are connecting with your Spirit. As a result, you can withstand your daily stresses with ease. You'll feel better knowing that you've taken care of yourself.

You are practicing radical self-love when you take time to conduct a daily dignity ritual.

I make time each day to treat myself with dignity, love and honor.

33. Reclaim Your Sexuality

You are sexy. It doesn't matter whether you look like the women on the cover of *Cosmo*. It doesn't matter if you are extra curvy in some places and not curvy enough in other places. Your sexiness comes from within.

We are so used to our definitions of what is sexy coming from the outside – celebrities, media, and the latest ads from Victoria's Secret. For the time being, suspend any outside notion of sexiness. Instead focus on *your* sexiness.

Go to a mirror. Now, flirt with yourself using just your eyes. Look at how mesmerizing you are! Look at that sparkle and shine. There is no one who can give that look quite like you!

Now, flirt using your mouth. Flirt with your mouth open. Flirt with it closed. Give yourself a flirty smile. Let your mouth exude sexiness and seduction.

Next, flirt using your heart. What does it feel like to flirt from your heart? Do you feel butterflies fluttering in your chest? Is there a glow that takes over your whole being when you flirt from your heart? Notice how flirting from your heart changes your posture.

Finally, flirt using your whole soul. Let your sexiness be like a magnet that radiates out 50 feet in all directions. You have a magnetism that is undoubtedly sexy and authentically you.

You are practicing radical self-love when you realize that your sexiness doesn't have to look like or feel like anyone else's sexiness. Your sexiness is innately in you!

I am innately sexy. My sexiness is beautiful, unique, and divine!

34. Your Sexuality Deserves to be Respected

We are all different and we have different sexual desires. That is a normal part of the human experience. Some women have low levels of sexual desire, while others have a high level. Whatever your experience with your sexuality, it is perfect. Sexuality is on a spectrum. It starts in the mind and moves into a physical, emotional, and spiritual experience.

Are you fully aware of what pleases you? Have you taken the time to explore your sexuality using all five senses? Do you allow yourself to fantasize and learn what turns you on? Do you take the time to discuss what you really want from your lover?

Part of fully claiming your sexuality is to give yourself permission to learn what you want and to feel deserving enough to ask for it. I'm not talking about what the media or society thinks you should want. I'm talking about what YOU really want. How do you want to be kissed? What kind of touch feels good to you? Do you prefer to be pursued or to chase? What does romance mean to you? How important is romance for you? Really take the time to explore this. We live in a society where we are bombarded with images of sex and sexuality, yet very few people consciously explore what is important to them.

You are practicing radical self-love when you take the time to learn what you really enjoy with respect to your sexuality, ask for it, and know that you deserve to receive it.

I am aware of what pleases me sexually and I deserve to have my sexual desires met. I love and trust myself enough to ask for what I want and to receive it.

35. Balance your Feminine and Masculine Energies

Each of us has both masculine energy and feminine energy. The degrees to which we embody each of these energies may differ; nevertheless, all of us have both and we need both.

Masculine energy generally consists of action and doing. It includes such attributes as looking outward and being hard, firm, logical, strong, rational, rough, and loud. Feminine energy is an energy of being. It includes such attributes as receptivity, intuition, nurturing, sensitivity, delicateness, emotional, and looking inward.

We live in an era and society that celebrates masculine energy and devalues feminine energy. We receive awards and accolades for what we do and accomplish. We don't get recognized for just *being*. In fact, most of the time, we are criticized for taking the time out to just be. The art of being is so devalued that most people have a hard time getting still. When they start to get quiet, they get antsy.

It is time to reclaim more of your feminine energy. There is great value in just being. It is in being that things are truly able to be born. It is the place where you can readily access your intuition and your imagination. When you harness the power of your divine feminine energy and balance it with the action-oriented nature of your divine masculine energy, you invite more ease and joy into your life.

You are practicing radical self-love when you honor and balance your masculine and feminine energies.

I balance my masculine and feminine energies. I take the time I need to be still and connect with my divinity. From this grounded place, I move into action until it is time to be still again.

36. Radically Accept Your Sexuality

Part of radical self-love includes radical self-acceptance of your sexuality. This means fully embracing your sexuality. I am not just talking about your sexual orientation – I am talking about fully allowing yourself to have intimacy with your sexuality – to stay connected to your body and spirit.

Most women (especially survivors of sexual assault, molestation, or incest) either underplay or overemphasize their sexuality. This is, in part, because of the messages and stereotypes we receive about our sexuality as women. But, neither extreme is loving. What IS loving is to embrace the fact that our sexuality is an expression of, and a portal for, our divine energy. As a result, we must act on our sexuality from a place of integrity.

To begin developing an intimate connection to your sexuality, think about your own sexual history. What are the images and messages about sex and intimacy that really appeal to you? When did you feel most present in your body and spirit during a sexual encounter? When have you felt the least connected? How do you feel about sex? How do you feel about your body? Does sex make you feel vulnerable? Really explore your relationship with your sexuality.

You are practicing radical self-love when you fully examine and embrace your sexuality. Once you do, you can take steps to engage in more things that help you stay present and connected during sex, while mitigating the things that keep you feeling disconnected.

I fully embrace and accept my sexuality. It is a source of pleasure and a way in which I can connect with myself and another with love and harmony.

37. Take Yourself Out on a Date

Begin a love affair with yourself! Court yourself. In your mind's eye, you have fantasies about how you'd like to be wooed. Well, start to woo yourself.

Maybe you wanted your sweetheart to bring you fresh flowers each week or surprise you with a date at a lovely restaurant. Maybe you always wanted to receive love letters. Whatever it is that you wished from another, start doing it for yourself. You don't need to wait for anyone else to give you what you long for. In fact, when you decide to start loving and caring for yourself in this way, you are increasing your vibration around the love you receive. You will attract more experiences of loving kindness as a result of this higher vibration.

It's funny how many of us will bend over backwards for those who we love, but we are so reluctant to do it for ourselves. Aren't you worthy of your own love and affection? Aren't you worth your time? Before you can truly love another person, you have got to love yourself. If you don't, you won't know what love is. You will attract unloving experiences. You will attract co-dependent relationships. You will put too much pressure on an intimate relationship to fulfill your needs when, really, you are responsible for fulfilling your own needs.

You are practicing radical self-love when you take the time to date yourself. Go all out!

I am the love that I seek. I am beautiful and sexy and divine. I long to be in the presence of my own company. I take the time to intimately get to know me and I am rapt with attention at my every word, thought and action!

38. Sex is Safe

One out of every three women have been sexually assaulted or molested. Let me repeat that. One out of every three women have been sexually assaulted or molested. This can have a devastating impact on our sexuality, not just as survivors of sexual violence, but as women as a whole through our shared collective consciousness. Think about mothers, grandmothers, aunts, sisters, friends, and partners who may have unwittingly passed on their fears and doubts around sexuality because of their personal experience with sexual violence.

It's time to reclaim sex. Sex is a divine gift in which women are meant to experience pleasure. But before we can, we have to realize that sex can be safe.

Turn to the divine within and answer the following questions. What does a healthy sex life look like for you? What are the boundaries you can create in order to allow your body, mind and spirit the freedom to experience sexual ecstasy? What do you need to heal in order to feel safe with sex again?

Radical self-love means taking the time to heal whatever wounds exist with respect to your sexuality and fully reclaiming your sexuality.

I know that sex is safe. I choose partners and activities that always create a satisfying and safe sexual experience.

39. Your Womb is Powerful

The womb is a sacred space within the belly of a woman, regardless of whether she has her uterus or not. It carries great spiritual significance. A woman's womb is the center of her power and creativity. To fully access your divine feminine power, you must tend to your womb.

We have been taught to disregard our womb. The only time most of us pay any attention to our womb is when we are pregnant, trying to get pregnant or menstruating. And even then, many of us have come to hate or resent these aspects of our femininity because of the pain, discomfort, or messiness of it. Rather than recognizing and connecting with our wombs as a source of sacred power, we distance ourselves from it.

You can reclaim greater creative power and strength if you start rejuvenating your relationship with your womb. You can harness the power of the natural cyclical energy of the womb, which literally and spiritually can bring forth all that needs to be cleansed and healed. You can have more strength in creating the life that you envision by establishing a stronger relationship with your womb.

This may sound crazy to you. If it does, don't worry. It only appears crazy because of our society's devaluation of the sacred feminine. Try to keep an open mind.

To begin establishing a healthier relationship with your womb, simply engage in a daily, five-minute meditation. While lying down, place your hands on your lower belly in an upside-down triangular shape. Focus your attention on your womb. Send your womb love and light as you inhale and exhale. This simple daily meditation can help heal old wounds, clear out negative energies from your sexual history, and open you up to receive more and create more.

You are practicing radical self-love when you recognize that your womb is a source of sacred feminine power. It, and all that it does, is a gift. Treat your womb with love and respect.

It is my divine right to fully access the sacred power of my womb — the source of creation, power and healing. I love and accept my beautiful womb.

40. Spirit-Filled Sex

Sex can be a gateway to experience Spirit. Spirit is expansive. It is free and the greatest expression of love. When we make love, we have the capacity to feel the expansiveness of Spirit.

If we allow it, sex can become a great teacher of things that we tend to have trouble experiencing in our everyday lives. When we are in a loving sexual encounter, we know how to surrender and let go. We allow ourselves to experience ecstasy. We allow ourselves to release tension and experience relaxation. We are able to connect in love with another person. We are able to be of service to them when we pleasure them. We know how to give and to receive. We have the ability to feel safe, secure, and content. We allow ourselves to be playful and carefree.

When we allow ourselves to fully feel the power of love-making, we are connecting with Spirit. We are given a glimpse of the pure joy, expansiveness, trust, and surrender that is Divine Love.

You are practicing radical self-love when you allow yourself to have sexual encounters that are Spirit-filled. Sex can be a sacred act that becomes a portal to understanding and experiencing the vast expanse of love.

I am fully present when I make love. I allow myself to experience my sexual encounter as a glimpse of the expansiveness of Spirit. I give. I receive. I trust. I surrender. I expand. I feel the oneness. I am in bliss.

AFFIRMATIONS
FOR YOUR

41. Refuse to Numb Yourself

There is no doubt about it. Life can be painful at times. It can be too much at times. And those of us who are on a path of personal and spiritual growth (as you are) will tend to want to get off this course because sometimes, it is just too damned hard.

When you are going through a tough time, it's easy to want to numb out. Numbing out is simply choosing to do things that will stop you from feeling your feelings. We numb ourselves in a variety of ways. We could become obsessed with food, work, the kids, television, shopping, the house, working out, etc. We could turn to alcohol or drugs. It doesn't matter what you choose as your vehicle for numbing yourself from the intensity of life. The point is that when you consistently choose to numb yourself, you deprive yourself from an opportunity to truly heal.

When you find yourself reaching for something to "take the edge off," take a minute to pause. Investigate what the underlying feelings are that you're trying to avoid. Know that your mind and your Spirit would not give you more than you can truly handle. Trust your ability to handle whatever is before you. Ask the Divine to support you in your effort to address the situation head on.

You are practicing radical self-love whenever you choose to deal with the situation or feeling rather than numb it.

I choose to stay present to my experience, knowing that I am fully capable of handling whatever is before me. I trust that the Divine gives me only that which I can handle.

42. Take Time to Notice the Joy

Do you tend to notice what has not yet been accomplished? Are you constantly focused on what you (or others) could do better? If so, you may be viewing the world through only one lens.

You were given the ability to see the lack so that you could use it as a jumping off point to learn from it and grow. It serves an important purpose. But, if all you do is stay focused on the lack, the broken, and imperfections, then that is all you will attract. Instead, use what you notice as lack as an opportunity to reframe and reclaim what you truly want.

In *every* moment, there is both abundance and lack. Start taking time to notice what is abundant in your life. Notice the joy in your life. Notice when someone offers you a smile. Notice how green the grass is. Notice all the little things that are ever present.

What are some of the amazing things that happen in your life that you take for granted? Begin a gratitude journal – a book dedicated solely to all the great things – big and small – that you appreciate. The Universe is generous. It gives you more of what you focus your attention on.

You are practicing radical self-love by taking the time to notice all that there is to be grateful and joyous about, and connecting with the positive feelings that these things bring you.

I love myself enough to notice and appreciate everything that brings me joy!

43. Accept Your Emotional Being

Radical self-love requires you to accept your emotional being. Part of accepting our emotional being is recognizing that we experience a painful emotion (anger, sadness, shame, etc.) so that we can fully appreciate its opposite. You would not really know joy if you haven't experienced pain. You cannot fully cultivate compassion if you have never experienced shame.

Many times, people don't want to deal with their painful emotions. Rather than dealing with it, they stuff their emotions and choose to do things that would numb themselves. But, it is really important to allow yourself to completely feel your emotions. By feeling them, you allow them to be released. When you are willing to give yourself the time and space to face your emotions, you'll realize that the experience is far less scary than what you imagined it to be.

You cannot rid yourself of pain; but, you can work to reduce the intensity with which you feel it. One way to reduce the intensity is to accept and compassionately pay attention to the wounded parts of you (whether it's a wounded child, teenager, or adult). By doing so, you decrease the chance that those parts will create unpleasant situations that force you to pay attention to it.

You are practicing radical self-love when you allow yourself to experience and process all of your emotions.

I am an emotional being; therefore, I choose to welcome and deal with each of my emotions thoroughly and compassionately.

44. Get the Support You Need

We are not meant to do it all by ourselves! Yet, that's exactly what many of us do. We think we are absolutely alone. We don't trust others to help. We refuse to delegate. We refuse to get help. It's time to change that!

Getting the support you need cuts short the time it takes to heal, grow, evolve, and accomplish your ultimate goals. Receiving support doesn't mean that you are weak; it means you are strong and wise.

There are a number of avenues of support. For your emotional being, consider a therapist or a life coach to help you release old unhealthy patterns so that you can move forward easily. For your physical health, you can work with a nutritional counselor, personal chef, or personal trainer. For an addiction, there are specific support groups like Alcoholics Anonymous, Codependents Anonymous, Overeaters Anonymous, etc. If the group you are looking for doesn't exist, dare to create it. For your spirit, find a spiritual community you can belong to. If you are moved by nature, then find a hiking club or some other group where you will be out in nature. There are so many ways in which we can rest on the shoulders of another as we propel forward.

Once you get the right type of support, really play full out. Commit. Take action. Go consistently to your source of support. Be open and honest with your support team. Do the work required of you. Celebrate your successes. Lean on your support team when your attempts have failed.

You are practicing radical self-love when you find the support you need and utilize it fully.

I am never alone. I am surrounded by the love and support I need.

45. Deal with Unresolved Anger

When you have unresolved underlying anger, it shows up in various ways. You can become the exact person that you detest. You can turn the anger inward and begin to hate yourself and act in self-destructive ways.

Anger is not a bad thing. It is a powerful energy that needs to be released responsibly! Anger is a secondary emotion. Meaning, it is an emotion that envelopes the underlying primary emotion. It is like a protective shield that guards against the inner, more vulnerable, emotions – emotions such as feeling unloved, hurt, sadness, disappointment, rejection, pain, etc.

Most people avoid their own anger because they are afraid of it. They refuse to let it come up. This often means that they also refuse to address the underlying primary emotion. When you fail to deal with your emotions fully and responsibly, your anger will be abused.

Do not judge yourself for your anger. Treat yourself with love and compassion, even with respect to your anger. To help you deal with your anger, try the following meditation:

> Take a deep breath and set the intention to be free from your anger. Ask the Divine to show you vividly and clearly the source of your anger. Allow the anger to come up fully, knowing that you are safe and protected. Observe your anger and the situations that caused it. Notice what emotions are beneath your anger. What was the vulnerability that your anger was trying to protect? Offer what you needed at that time to yourself. Say what you wished you had said. Do what you wished you could have done. Now, offer love and forgiveness

to yourself and the others involved. Imagine that the whole situation releases into the air like a hot air balloon.

Anytime you find yourself getting angry, ask yourself, "What does this situation remind me of?" Then repeat the meditation. Repeat this meditation as often as you need to completely release your anger. Remember, your release will happen in layers. Do not get discouraged if you continue to have residuals from your anger. Trust the process. Trust that you are peeling away the layers of your anger.

You are practicing radical self-love when you take the time to reflect on and release your anger. It will leave you in layers and ultimately, with consistent practice, you will be free.

I am completely safe and I now choose to acknowledge and release any anger that is trapped inside me. It is released and I am free!

46. Understanding Frustration

Frustration is the disappointment you feel when your expectations are not met. You want something so badly and it's not manifesting. You keep trying to get that dream job and it doesn't happen. You keep trying to make your relationship work, and you still fight. You keep trying to lose weight, and the scale isn't budging.

When you start to feel frustrated, take a step back and breathe. Do you realize what is really going on here? Control. You are trying so hard to control things that are outside of your control and your role in the Universe.

Here is your role. You are a co-creator with the Universe. What this means is that you get to visualize what you want. You have the responsibility to continue to hold on to that vision, and eliminate any thoughts that do not serve you. When you see the disappointments and frustrations arise, it is a gift. It is showing you the blocks in your subconscious, and you get an opportunity to work on it. Only these things are in your control. When and how things manifest are not in your control.

To eliminate the frustration, surrender it to God. Keep doing your part dutifully and faithfully. It will manifest. Know that God is looking at things from a much bigger and more complete picture. From our limited view, it may appear as if we know when things should occur, but we don't always know. Instead, surrender and trust in the divine timing of things.

You are practicing radical self-love when you realize God is always on your side.

I am a powerful co-creator with the Universe. My vision will manifest at exactly the right time and in the perfect way.

47. You are Not a Failure

You are not a failure. Just because your actions toward a particular outcome did not succeed does not make you a failure. It means an event occurred that didn't go the way you had hoped it would. The key is to not take that event and pretend that it is an indication of who you are.

Feel disappointment about the event, but resist the urge to turn yourself into a failure. It's impossible for you to be a failure. You are one with the Divine. Could you imagine calling God a failure or a loser? Well, that's just how ridiculous it is to call yourself a failure!

You are supposed to make mistakes. Things are not supposed to always work out the way you want them to. And sometimes, the failures happen for an extended period of time. All of these events are just opportunities for you to continue to learn and grow so you can be a freer and more expanded version of yourself. Every failed event leads you one step closer toward your goal.

When you experience a failure, what can you learn about yourself? Look for patterns of behaviors. For example, do you tend to handle yourself with love and compassion or harshness? If you are typically harsh with yourself, each "failure" is an invitation to learn to go through the inevitable "downs" of life in a more loving and compassionate way.

You are practicing radical self-love when you realize that each failed event is an opportunity to become your best self, which can never turn you – the divine being that you are – into a failure.

I accept my failures with love and compassion toward myself.

48. You Will Expand and Contract

Your personal growth journey is much like a heartbeat -- it expands and contracts. The contraction is the stillness needed to propel you into the next period of expansion. You need to rest throughout your evolutionary journey. It is a time when you get to build up your reserves, be quiet and reflect, and allow the voice of the Divine and your own spirit to guide you to the next level.

Many times when we are in a contracted space, we feel like something is wrong with us. We immediately judge the situation as bad. We hate being in a valley! Maybe the contraction shows up as less motivation to get things done. Perhaps it shows up as melancholy. Maybe you lack energy. Whatever the contraction period is, know that it is not a permanent state. Even if it lasts a while. The most important thing is to not judge it. Allow it to naturally move from a place of stillness to one of action.

You are practicing radical self-love when you trust in the process of your emotions. It comes up in waves. Your mind is careful not to give you more than you can handle at any one moment. If you trust in the process of your emotions, you will evolve at the perfect time and rate for you. And, you can enjoy the journey rather than judging and condemning yourself for the periods of contraction.

I trust in the natural rhythm of my emotions, knowing that whenever I am in a period of contraction, it is giving me the strength and rest I need to propel and expand.

49. Become the Parent that You Never Had

For many of us, our parents have done things that have caused us harm. They may have abandoned you, been emotionally unavailable to you, crossed physical boundaries with you, or worse. It doesn't necessarily mean that they are bad people. They have done the very best that they could given what's been done to them and what they know.

Although you can't change who your parents are and what has been done to you, you can have your needs met by becoming the parents you never had. You can give yourself all that you needed from them.

Start by getting in touch with the little girl inside of you. What was she longing for from her parent(s)? If you are having difficulty knowing what you needed at the time, ask the Divine to help you make a conscious connection with your younger self. Writing with your dominant hand, ask her what she wanted from her parents/guardians. Then, with your non-dominant hand, have her respond to you.

Once you discover what it is that she needed, start developing ways for you to nurture her and provide her with the things she longs for. For example, if she longed to have more of her mother's attention, then decide to spend a few minutes every day giving the little girl inside of you attention. Go for a walk with her. Listen to her stories. Play. Each time you give the little girl in you what she longed for from her parents, you heal.

You are practicing radical self-love when you parent yourself, giving yourself everything that you longed for.

I thank my parents and guardians for being my spiritual teachers. I trust in my ability to heal my childhood wounds and I now give myself the unconditional love, acceptance, and attention that I needed from them.

50. Laugh Out Loud

Who said the road to personal growth has to be all serious, filled with piety and solemn self-reflection? It doesn't! You are allowed to have fun. In fact, you are supposed to have fun.

There are so many benefits to laughter. Did you know that laughing can help you reduce pain, increase immunity, and decrease stress? In addition to these physical benefits, laughter also helps stimulate your intellectual and emotional functions. It helps us take ourselves less seriously and gain a new perspective on our trials and tribulations. Laughter can help us overcome fear and anxiety. In addition to being an antidote to ailments, laughter helps open up our creativity.

We are meant to experience joy. So, go ahead and laugh. Laugh a big belly laugh! Let that laughter heal you. Let it cleanse you. Let it bring up and release the old memories and hurts that are lodged in your muscles and bones.

You are practicing radical self-love when you let yourself laugh out loud.

I love to laugh! I laugh easily and heartily. I see the humor and joy in all things! All is well in my world.

51. Say What You Need to Say

How often have you kept your mouth shut because you didn't want to upset the other person or come across a certain way? Have you ever thought about the impact that your silence has on you?

You end up diminishing your relationship with yourself when you consistently silence yourself. You are signaling to yourself that the feelings and opinions of others outweigh your feelings and opinions.

A slogan during the AIDS epidemic stated, "Silence = Death." It does. Each time you silence yourself from expressing something genuinely important to you, you are killing off a piece of you. If you keep this up for a period of time, your Self will die. You will not know who you are. You will not have any opinions on things. You will not be putting anything out for the world to consider and learn from.

When you silence yourself, you are also demonstrating the greatness of your fear. Perhaps you are afraid of being rejected or creating tension. When you fail to stand up for yourself and say what you need to say, you not only deprive yourself of the opportunity to be true to yourself, but you also deprive the other person from experiencing genuine love and an opportunity for them to learn. When you're operating from a place of fear, love is not present. Fear is the opposite of love. As a result, love and fear cannot coexist at the same time.

You are practicing radical self-love when you have the courage to say what you need to say even when saying it may be difficult in the moment.

I act from the highest form of love toward myself and others when I dare to speak my truth on matters that are important to me.

52. Create Closure You Can Control

When a relationship ends, it's important to obtain closure. It's not always possible to have closure with the other person. If both parties are willing and able to have closure (either of the relationship or of a particular hurtful circumstance), it can be a cathartic experience. However, having closure with the other person is not realistic for a lot of people. Nevertheless, you can experience closure on your own, and it can be just as cathartic as if you did it with the other person.

To have closure that you can control, engage in a ritual that will help you experience closure (despite whether the other person grants you time or space for closure). Although symbolic in nature, rituals are very helpful for achieving closure. By experiencing a symbolic ending, you are making room for new possibilities. Some rituals you may want to try are:
- write a letter to the person (your choice on whether you send it to them or not)
- get rid of painful memorabilia
- visualize having a conversation with the person in which you fully express your feelings, and imagine that they attentively listen to you and acknowledge what you are expressing
- write the most painful things you've experienced on a piece of paper and throw it into the ocean or a fire pit

You are practicing radical self-love when you grant yourself the gift of closure even when the other person can't or won't.

I love myself enough to complete each relationship.

53. Forgive Those Who Have Hurt You

Contrary to popular belief, forgiveness is not just about the person who hurt you. The bigger part of forgiveness is the gift you give yourself. You get to let go — let go of the pain, hurt, and anger that you are holding on to because of the harm caused. You also get to let go of the energy and life force that the person and the situation are taking from you. Instead of using that energy to continue to fuel the flames of your past, you can use it to create the present and the future that you really want.

Forgiveness is also about accepting the person and the circumstance for what they truly are. Because you have to accept the fact that you are disappointed by the actions of another, you will have to go through a grieving process.

Forgiving someone is a process that occurs in stages. At first, your emotions are fresh. You are feeling the intensity of the hurt, pain, anger, and betrayal. You can't believe how you've been treated. Allow all the feelings to come up, but don't judge them.

Next, start to clearly identify what hurt you. What was it about the person's actions that caused you pain? Did you feel like your boundaries were violated? Did you feel like they failed to meet your expectation?

See if you could understand why the person behaved as they did. Did something happen to them that made it easy for them to hurt you? Do they lack the skills, emotional intelligence, or awareness of how their actions would have affected you? Although you are trying to exercise compassion, this does not mean that you are excusing the other person's behavior. This is simply to help you expand your own awareness about what might have occurred from the other person's perspective. By cultivating some compassion, it makes it easier for you to forgive and let go.

Focus on what you would gain if you could really let this go. Would you have more energy? Would you feel lighter? What would you do with the time you were spending perseverating on the situation?

Say what you need to say. You can do a visualization to accomplish this. Or you can actually speak with the individual.

Now, let go!

You are practicing radical self-love when you take the time to process your emotions until you can forgive another person for hurting you and let go of the negative energy.

I forgive [name of person] for [action that caused you harm]. I accept what happened, I acknowledge the lessons learned, and I release this situation with love.

54. Don't Try to Fix It

Picture this. Someone you care about comes to you to talk about something that they are frustrated about. After listening for a few minutes, you immediately try to "fix" the problem. You offer advice. You provide solutions. Yet, you notice that the other person is getting more withdrawn or anxious. What they really need is someone to just listen.

When you go into a "fix it" mode, chances are that there is something about the situation that triggers *you*. Maybe there is something about the subject matter or the emotional field that the others person is in that makes you uncomfortable. Perhaps they are in a space that you can't tolerate within yourself.

Here's an example to illustrate. Let's assume that your friend is crying. You personally hate to cry. You don't allow yourself to do it. So, when you see your friend cry, a part of you begins to "fix it" so that you don't have to tolerate what you are uncomfortable with. You trying to fix it is about YOU, unless they ask you to help fix it.

The next time you notice that you are trying to fix it or problem-solve something for another person without them asking you to, resist! Just listen. Later, when you are alone, reflect on what it was about the situation that might have triggered you.

You are practicing radical self-love when you resist the urge to solve other people's problems and use your experiences to further understand yourself.

I am now aware that when I try to fix it for another without being asked for help, there is something about the situation that I am too uncomfortable to be with. I now choose to use the situation to better understand myself and my triggers.

55. Bless It and End It

People come into our lives for a reason, a season, or a lifetime. Part of the reason why we attract people in our lives is because they are spiritual teachers for us and we are spiritual teachers for them. Meaning, we serve a true purpose in each other's lives.

But, often we try to hang on to someone long after the purpose has been served. When we do, it leads to great strife, chaos, and a depleted sense of self. Now, don't be confused. In most relationships, you will experience some degree of tension, fighting, strife and chaos. A certain level of this is necessary for your personal and spiritual growth. The problem occurs when it is chronic.

If you are in a relationship where you consistently, over a period of time, feel like the relationship is sucking the life out of you, you need to bless it and end it. If you consistently, over a period of time, leave conversations with a person feeling angry, bitter, lost, unloved, unlovable, or less than, it is time to walk away. If you feel at all confused about whether a relationship you are in is in the "healthy chaos" that makes you grow and expand versus the "unhealthy, no-longer-serving-me chaos," then it is time for you to get still and ask the Divine. But be forewarned, you may not like what you hear.

You are practicing radical self-love every time you have the courage to end a relationship that no longer serves you.

I am perfectly clear on which relationships serve me and I now choose to end any relationship that no longer does with love. I am grateful for the lessons learned and I bless the other person for being my spiritual teacher. With this ending, I make room for new people to contribute to my highest good.

56. Find Your Fun

Have you forgotten how to have fun? If so, now's the time to reignite your fun factor! Think about things that you've enjoyed doing – from childhood until now.

If you are not sure how to have fun, ask yourself the following questions:

- What did I enjoy doing when I was a child?
- What makes me feel good now?
- One thing that I heard someone else talk about that seemed interesting was . . .
- Secretly, I've always wanted to . . .

Start doing these things (even if that means playing with dolls or LEGOs!) and discover what it means to engage in these activities now. Keep an open mind and be willing to experiment. When you find something (or an aspect of something) that feels fun, keep doing it and find other similar things that you can do too.

You are practicing radical self-love when you make having fun a priority in your life. Spend time enjoying yourself. Laugh! Dance. Paint. Be silly. Whatever you do, just enjoy yourself.

I am so much fun! I love and enjoy my life!

57. It is Safe to Be Present

Have you ever watched a child play? They are fully present in the moment. If they happen to fall down while playing, they cry for a few minutes and then they move on. If they are happy, they have huge smiles on their faces. They have complete emotional authenticity.

As we grow up, we lose the ability to fully be emotionally authentic. Somewhere along the line we've learned that it is not safe to feel our feelings. So, we shut them down. Because our feelings are only available to us in the present, we've inadvertently learned that the present is not safe. Instead, we choose to focus on the past or on the future.

The present is safe. The present is what we make of it. We can choose to view anything that happens from an empowered perspective. Let's say you had a bad day at work. Allow yourself to be fully present to the experience. If you feel frustration, anger, judgment, shame – allow yourself to feel it completely. Don't hold back. You will notice that you will naturally emerge from the unhappy state into a natural state of peace.

You are practicing radical self-love when you recognize that the present is safe because it is always the result of how you interpret and respond to the moment. Remember, how you interpret a situation and how you respond to it is *always* within your control.

I trust that it is safe to be fully present and I allow myself to feel my emotions completely so that I may return to my natural state of joy.

58. Be Patient with Your Process

If there is one thing that we all have to learn, it's how to exercise greater patience. Yes, you want to get there – wherever "there" may be for you – but sometimes, you must meander. Sometimes, you must take detours. Know and trust that all that you do, including the lulls and detours, are there to serve you. You may not realize why things are taking longer than you think they should, but there is a higher purpose that is at work.

When you are not patient, you will resort to judgment. You will start to think that something is wrong with you or that your efforts weren't good enough. Instead of moving into judgment, develop compassion for yourself.

All you can do is take the next baby step. Move confidently in the direction of where you want to go, but focus only on the next immediate step. Getting to where you want to go takes time. And you need to be ready to actually receive what you are looking for.

Every blessing in our life requires a gestation period. Sometimes, the gestation period is short. Other times, it can take years. The point is, if we receive what we ask for before we are truly ready, it could be harmful. View the detours and lulls as part of your gestation period – a time when much is percolating on the inside, outside the purview of what you can consciously observe. Yet, if you move in the direction of your dreams with love and compassion for yourself, and have faith in the Divine, then you will receive what you seek at exactly the right time.

You are practicing radical self-love when you exercise patience for your process.

I am patient with myself and my process, knowing that all will happen in Divine time and in Divine order.

59. When You Want to Attract Love, Lead with Vulnerability

We desperately want love, but we are afraid to be vulnerable. Instead, we operate from a place of fear. We are afraid if the other person knows who we truly are, they won't love us. We're afraid that they will hurt us. We are afraid of being abandoned.

Fear does not beget love. Love begets love. Part of love is trusting that you are safe and allowing your vulnerability to show. People connect more easily with vulnerability than fear. Think about your own life. Isn't it easier for you to connect with someone when they are straightforward, even if that means that they may have exposed something fragile about themselves? Wouldn't you rather they tell you they are afraid or shy or concerned than shut you out because they are *operating* from those places rather than discussing and dealing with them?

Being vulnerable does not make you weak. In fact, it takes a great deal of strength. Of course, you are afraid to be vulnerable. It can be scary. You may have been hurt before. You feel exposed when you're vulnerable. But, you can rise above it in a safe way. Ask the Divine to vividly and clearly show you how you can feel safe while being vulnerable. Ask the Divine to reveal who you can be vulnerable with. Once you get a clear indication from the Divine, make the choice to operate from that place of love and refuse to be beholden to the fear of being hurt again.

You are practicing radical self-love when you make the conscious choice to be vulnerable with those you love and from whom you seek love.

I am safe being vulnerable with those whom I love.

60. Break the Unhealthy Patterns of Your Family

We inherit certain unhealthy patterns and behaviors from our families. Perhaps the women in your family are overweight and they carry shame about their bodies. And now, you carry shame about your body. Perhaps your family of origin dealt with anger with explosive outbursts or by withholding love. You now see how you repeat those patterns. Despite the long history of these patterns, you can break them.

The first step in breaking patterns that are unhealthy is noticing what the patterns are. To understand the patterns, conduct the following exercise:

> Take a deep breath. Set the intention to discover familial patterns that do not serve you. Make a conscious connection with your spirit. Now, ask the Divine to show you vividly and clearly what your family engaged in that caused you to dim your own light, shrink, or reduce your vibrance and vitality. Once you get a clear sense of some things, ask the Divine to show you how you might be continuing the patterns with yourself and with others. Now, ask the Divine what you should do to break these patterns.

You are practicing radical self-love when you get clear about the unhealthy patterns you have inherited from your family of origin, and commit to breaking those patterns. When you do, you allow more of your light and true essence to shine through.

I am now aware of the unhealthy patterns that I have inherited from my family. I release myself from these patterns and I take consistent action to create new healthy ways to allow my vibrance and those of others to fully shine!

61. Pain Will Not Break You

Oh what tangled webs we weave – especially to avoid pain! We will do just about anything to prevent feelings of pain. We avoid situations that we think will cause us pain. We numb ourselves with too much food, alcohol, drugs, television, work, or sex. We pretend that the pain is not there. But, it is.

There is pain lurking deep within the chambers of your heart, and it needs to be released. Yet, the more you resist dealing with it, the bigger, hairier and unmanageable it appears. That which you resist, persists. You believe that, like the wizard in the *Wizard of Oz*, your pain is omnipotent. You think it is larger and more powerful than it really is.

But it is just pain. And pain will not break you. Contrary to how you may feel, it will not kill you. It actually is an invitation to evolve. To become a greater version of you.

In order to release pain and have it transmute into a healthy growth experience, you must go through the pain. Greet your pain with love and compassion. Be very gentle and tender with yourself, yet detached enough that you do not become absorbed by your pain. Allow your pain to come up. This doesn't mean that you have to relive what caused you the pain. It simply means that you must give the pain a chance to be seen and heard. Observe it. As you do, you will notice that it will naturally begin to dissolve and evolve. Pain has its seasons and it will naturally enter its Winter – preparing you for the renewal of Spring -- if you allow it.

You are practicing radical self-love when you deal with your pain.

My spirit is larger than my pain. I face my pain directly, and with love and compassion, knowing that all is well.

62. Surviving Rejection

Rejection is a painful part of life that *everyone* faces at one time or another. All forms of rejection hurt, but when someone you love rejects you, it can be devastating. Maybe you were spurned by your partner or lover. Maybe you feel rejected because your parents don't accept you for who you are or for the choices you made. Perhaps a close friend has "kicked you to the curb" for a new friend or because they are in love.

When you are rejected by someone you really love, it can be damaging to your spirit and your self-esteem. You are in "The Dip" – that inevitable low feeling that makes you feel like you are less than zero. When you are in The Dip it can be difficult to bounce back and feel normal again.

When there is a disruption in one of our key relationships, most of us take the loss personally. We internalize the circumstances and revise our inner dialogue to include feelings of abandonment, shame, guilt, rejection, unworthiness, blame, and judgment. To "internalize" means to take in the information and make a personal association with it, usually integrating that information into your own beliefs and attitudes.

You are practicing radical self-love when you realize that rejection is a normal part of life, and it's a necessary step in the creation of happiness. Each rejection helps us get clearer about what we truly want.

I accept that I may face rejection from time to time. When I feel rejected, I choose to use the information to learn more about myself and to powerfully create what I want. The circumstances that caused me to feel rejected cannot change the truth – that I am worthy, loved, and capable!

63. Create a Timeline of Your Life

So much has happened to you! There have been triumphs and hardships. There have been periods of expansion and lulls. You have shed tears and you have laughed out loud. Each of these precious moments has shaped who you are.

To truly understand yourself and what makes you tick, make a timeline of the most significant events of your life. Grab a sheet of paper and draw a horizontal line on it. The line represents the years you've lived so far, starting with your birth and ending with where you are today. Begin to plot the most significant events in your life. Things that shaped you. Allow yourself plenty of time to let the memories come up.

Once your timeline feels complete, take a look at it as a whole. Look at your life with fresh eyes. What patterns do you notice? Can you pinpoint when and why you developed the behaviors you currently have? Is there anything that you currently do as a reaction to something that happened in your past? If so, is it time to let it go?

By creating a timeline of your life, you can start to get a more holistic view of what makes you you.

You are practicing radical self-love when you take the time to look at your complete history as a means of learning more about yourself and releasing any old habits, patterns and reactions that were created as a result of something that occurred in your past.

Today, I start anew. I take the lessons from my past and soar into the future!

64. Create and Maintain Healthy Personal Boundaries

One of the key elements of self-care and improving your sense of self-worth is to establish healthy personal boundaries. A personal boundary is a mental, emotional, or physical construct that defines the area in which you are willing to operate. When you have healthy boundaries, you are able to distinguish your own thoughts and feelings from those of others. Healthy personal boundaries protect you from being manipulated, controlled, or violated by others.

There are a number of things you can do to help create and maintain healthy personal boundaries. First, identify your personal values. What are the qualities and characteristics that are important to you? Examples are integrity, punctuality, honesty, and connection.

Once you're clear about your values, clarify your expectations of others. Think about how you want others to treat and speak to you. Then communicate your expectations clearly and consistently. Yes, you will have to repeat yourself at times. Communicating your boundaries is an ongoing process. Don't be afraid to communicate any new boundaries that come up over time.

Take action when someone violates your boundaries. This is a crucial step. For example, say "no" to any request that violates your personal boundaries or otherwise dishonors your values. Or, remind the person when a behavior is unacceptable to you.

You are practicing radical self-love when you set and maintain healthy personal boundaries.

I know who I am, what I value, where I begin and where I end. I choose relationships that honor my boundaries, and respect myself enough to let others lovingly know when they cross the line.

65. Enjoy the Process of Growing

So many times when we experience a growing pain, we think something is wrong with us. There is nothing wrong with you! Just because you went through a growing pain doesn't mean that you had something that needed to be "fixed." No, you are already wonderful and capable and glorious. Your experience is part of a process that is designed to help you fine-tune that which already exists in you. It's not about you missing something and needing to get it.

You cannot escape growing pains. It is a natural part of life. Bad things didn't happen to you to punish you. They happen to give you an opportunity to expand – to make what is already in you shine brighter.

You are practicing radical self-love when you accept that growing pains happen in your life not because you were bad and you deserve to be punished, but because you are so loved and because the Divine believes in you enough to know that you are ready for the next level.

I lovingly accept that growing pains are a natural part of life, and I choose to focus on the abundance I receive from the lesson rather than temporary feeling of lack produced by the pain.

AFFIRMATIONS FOR YOUR

66. Redesign Your Life

If you are lucky enough to breathe for the next 365 days, then you will have lived one year of life. The choice is whether you live a life that you design or one by default. Living a life by design is when you consciously choose the direction toward which you want your life to move.

Living a life by default is when you allow things to happen, without consciously directing your thoughts or efforts toward what you want. This happens when you hear yourself say things like, "Why does this always happen to me? I never get any breaks." Living a life by default also occurs when you live without consciousness or by what other people want.

It's important to note that to live a life by design you must decide on what *you* authentically want. What makes *your* heart sing? What would make you want to jump out of bed each morning? If you didn't have to worry about money, what other people thought, social status, or anything else, what would your life look like? If you can get a clear picture of what this life would look like, then you are taking the first step toward living a life by design.

Let me be clear, even when you consciously choose to live a life by design, it doesn't mean that everything will be smooth sailing. It's still life – which means, you will still have ups and downs. But, you know where you are headed, and each step you take (even the side steps that you take to deal with an unexpected turn of events) leads you closer to the vision you have for yourself.

You are practicing radical self-love when you consciously choose to live a life that you design.

I consciously co-create my life with the Divine, choosing to welcome only that which makes my heart sing.

67. Become a Life Activist

I dare you to become a life activist. A life activist is someone who is so passionate and devoted to their life that they take action in the direction of their dreams. They refuse to be a passive bystander with respect to their lives.

Have you ever watched or been part of a march or rally? Do you see the fervor with which the participants fight for their cause? They will go on strike, abstain from food, march for hours, and get arrested, all so that they can advance their cause. Well, I am asking you to take the same zeal and fervor that an activist has for a cause and apply it to your life!

If there is something you don't like about yourself or your life, commit to changing it. Dedicate the time necessary to make it happen. Develop a plan of action to make sure that you are victorious. Enlist the support of others. When setbacks occur, regroup. When you achieve a victory – no matter how small – celebrate. This is what an activist does for their cause. And this is what you can do for your life. Frankly, there is no cause greater than having a life that you love that allows you to be your absolute best, and share your gifts with others.

You are practicing radical self-love when you realize that you must fight to have the life that you truly want, and you commit to that fight, no matter what obstacles present themselves along the way.

I am an activist on behalf of my own life, fighting to have the most meaningful life I can conceive.

68. Silence Your Inner Critic

Inside each of us resides a harsh critic. It fills our mind with negative thoughts about ourselves. You may not even realize that it's talking. It's chatter may feel like the hum of a multitude of voices in a crowded restaurant. And yet, its messages penetrate to the depths of your being. It tells you things like, "Who do you think you are?" "You're not good enough." "You're not smart enough." "You're not attractive."

Your inner critic is hyper-vigilant in finding all the possible ways things could go wrong. Although its original purpose may have been to prevent you from experiencing hurt at the hands of others (for example, by preventing you from getting into situations where others may criticize or reject you), it has gone too far.

In order to silence your inner critic, you must first become aware of what it is saying. Once you're aware of it, you will be able to contradict its statements with a statement that is true, yet more loving of yourself. Your inner critic responds very well to logic. Therefore, it's crucial that you find facts and evidence that contradict your inner critic's statements. By presenting it with evidence to the contrary, you weaken the strength of its proclamation. But, be persistent. If your inner critic continues to bombard you with the same sentiment, and you only present the evidence to the contrary once in a while, then it will take longer to truly defeat your inner critic. Instead, create a practice of refuting your inner critic.

You are practicing radical self-love whenever you take the time to gather evidence that contradict the statements of your inner critic.

I refute the lies of my inner critic and replace them with the truth.

69. Detox Your Mind

The human mind thinks between 15,000-60,000 thoughts each day. Unfortunately, most of these thoughts tend to be toxic. A toxic thought is anything that erodes your self-esteem, drains your life energy, or condemns another. These thoughts tend to create negative feelings inside of you.

Imagine that each toxic thought literally deposits a toxic substance into your body. In essence it is. Studies have shown a link between the dis-ease of the mind and disease of the body.

The good news is that you can detoxify your mind by challenging your negative thoughts. With a little effort, you can convert negative thoughts into positive ones.

Think about a toxic thought that you tend to say to yourself frequently. Perhaps it's about your appearance, your intelligence, or your status. Spend a few minutes examining your thoughts. Write them down. On a scale of 1-10 (with 10 being the highest), how harsh are these thoughts?

For each thought, ask yourself, "Is there another way for me to look at this that feels better and also feels true?" Write down these new thoughts. Using the same 1-10 scale, re-evaluate how harsh this new thought is. By simply tweaking your toxic thoughts to those that feel better and are less harsh, you are gradually decreasing the toxicity in your mind and inevitably your body too.

You are practicing radical self-love when you commit to regularly taking time to weed out toxic thoughts and replace them with better feeling, life-affirming thoughts.

I am the master of my mind and I choose which thoughts I will believe.

70. You are More Powerful than Your Past

There may have been things in your past that really hurt you. It could've been a defining moment in your life. But, you are more powerful than your past.

Your mind strives to protect you from being hurt again. In doing so, it may be inadvertently limiting you based on what has happened in the past. You are trying so hard to not be hurt or have a similar experience again. So, you prevent yourself from ever being in a similar type of situation again. Maybe you choose not to be in a committed relationship. Or you choose to be guarded because you don't feel like you can trust people.

Your past is only an experience. It is something that occurred in the past. You can choose to not let it control your present and future. But, the choice is yours. What is the lesson you were supposed to learn from that experience? How do you need to show up differently? By taking the time to figure out what the lesson was from the experience, you release yourself from being beholden to it. You give your mind permission to know that you will not be hurt again in the same way because you have grown from the experience; you have not by avoided it.

You are practicing radical self-love when you trust that you are able to learn your lessons from your past and refuse to be beholden to it.

I am more powerful than my past and I choose to learn the lessons that my past experiences intended to teach me.

71. Stop Judging Yourself

You judge yourself thousands of times a day. "I'm too tired." "I'm too disorganized." "I can't seem to get anything right." "What I did wasn't good enough." STOP IT!

Your inner critic is relentless. Its messages are toxic to your wellbeing, your spirit, and your ability to create a magnificent life. Pretend you are a bouncer at a night club. You must stand guard at the door of your mind to make sure that you don't let these thoughts come in. If you notice that they are inside you, go in and pull them out.

The best way to stop your inner critic is to first notice what it is saying to you. Really get clear on its messages. Maybe you don't hear the words at first; maybe you just know that you feel crappy. Well, take time to get quiet and hear what your inner critic is saying to you. Then, ask yourself whether that statement is 100% true. If it isn't, start looking for evidence that disproves the statement.

Your inner critic is deeply steeped in its beliefs, but that is because it hasn't been challenged. When you take the time to show evidence that its statements are not accurate, you will be victorious over your inner critic.

You are practicing radical self-love by vigilantly standing guard at the door of your mind and ensuring that no inner critic gets in, and pulling them out when they sneak in.

I now choose to bring awareness to what I think, and I allow only thoughts that nourish my wellbeing and spirit to take residence in my mind.

72. Take 100% Responsibility for Your Life

Taking 100% responsibility for your life means that you acknowledge that you are responsible for your emotions, happiness, actions, and decisions. This means that you can't blame someone else if you are unhappy with all or parts of your life. The life you have was entrusted to *you*. You are the one who is responsible for ensuring that it's a life that you enjoy.

Your happiness does not lie in the hands of someone other than you. Contrary to what we're led to believe, no one else can make you happy. Your happiness is completely within your control. Other people's actions can have an impact on you. But, the choice is always yours as to how you will interpret and respond to the situation.

How can you start taking full responsibility for your life? First, know what you want. Second, notice whether you give someone else the power to make you happy. Do you blame your parents for how they reared you? Are you secretly hoping your partner will make you happy? Do you keep thinking that you will be happy at some future time, once you get the perfect job, reach your goal weight, or create the perfect family? If so, then you are giving away your power.

You are practicing radical self-love when you choose to take 100% responsibility for your life and stop blaming others for "causing" your unhappiness.

I accept full responsibility for my own happiness, actions, reactions, and decisions.

73. Your Thoughts Create Your Feelings

Whether we realize it or not, our thoughts create our feelings. To illustrate, imagine this scenario: You are frantically looking through a stack of papers for an important document. You think to yourself, "Ugh! What's wrong with me? I can never find anything!" If you thought that, how would you feel? Frustrated? Annoyed? Angry? Instead, imagine that you think, "I know it's here somewhere. I'm sure it's going to show up." Now, how would you feel? Calmer than the first set of thoughts, right?

Oftentimes, we don't pay attention to the thoughts in our heads. We're more likely to recognize a feeling. But sometimes, we have a tendency to take how we feel about a situation and imagine that it is a statement of who we are. For example, "I feel stupid, so I must be stupid." This is called emotional reasoning. When we reason from our emotions, we are engaging in a distorted thinking pattern.

In order to get to the real culprit behind your negative feelings, you have to examine what you are thinking. Notice when you first started feeling the way that you did. What happened? What kinds of things were you telling yourself or, if you can't remember, might you have said to yourself? Pinpoint the thoughts that are creating the emotional disturbance. Once you do, you can work to redirect your thinking to a more positive thought.

You are practicing radical self-love when you realize that your emotions are dictated by your thoughts; not the other way around. Know that you can always change your thoughts to something that makes you feel better.

I choose thoughts that produce positive emotions.

74. Know Your Values

When you know what your core values are, you can make decisions that help honor those values. A personal value is a quality or characteristic that is important to the individual who holds it. Examples include punctuality, respect, and integrity. Remember, these values are personal to you. They are not the values of society, your parents, or anyone else. To the extent that you share values with these outside figures, that's fine, but take the time to ensure that your values are genuinely yours.

To understand what your personal values are, do the following:
1. Think of a time when you were in a situation that really upset or angered you. Write down what specifically made you upset. This helps you identify circumstances when your values were dishonored. Name the values that were being dishonored. If you're having trouble coming up with the value, write down the exact opposite behavior of what bothered you.
2. Think of a specific moment when things were going well in your life. What was going on? What were you doing? Who was around? What felt right? These questions help you define a time when your values were being honored. Name the values that were being honored.

You are practicing radical self-love when you take the time to get to know what your personal value system is so that you can live by those values consistently.

I love and honor myself by being true to my personal values!

75. Dealing with Painful Mistakes

Life has moments that are fairly pleasant – sometimes they are surface-level; other times they are intimate. But in an instant, you can make a mistake that can change the pleasantries into something that is excruciatingly painful.

In that pain, there is no other place to go, but to turn inward. Your mistakes and mishaps are not without purpose. Each mistake or mishap that occurs in your life presents an opportunity for you to grow closer to your Soul and remember your divine essence. What is the lesson here for you? What was the mistake here to teach you?

You are not just your mistakes! Don't start berating yourself just because you made a mistake. It happens! The most important thing is to learn from it. Be loving with yourself. If it were a little girl who had made a mistake, how would you treat her? Wouldn't you be loving and compassionate? Wouldn't you want her to know that her mistake is not the sum of who she is? It is only an event.

Sometimes, even when the mistake passes, its effects linger. It continues to sting and be visible. Don't be discouraged by that. Trust in the healing process and *know* that the pain will go away, revealing a brighter, more magnificent you!

You are practicing radical self-love when you treat yourself with love, compassion and without judgment for the mistakes you have made, and learn from them.

I am more than my mistakes! My mistakes are here to show me where I can learn to love myself more deeply and evolve into all that I can be!

76. Declutter Your Space

Clutter in your environment can represent the manifestation of clutter in the mind. It breeds stagnation. It takes up space, leaving no room for what is new. It absorbs energy. And, it represents a lack mentality.

How could clutter represent lack, when it appears to show abundance? It shows that you have a hard time letting go. You do not believe that what you need will return to you when you need it. In other words, you do not trust the Universe to be there for you.

To help you get to the root cause of this and release you from your clutter, think of your earliest memory of feeling abandoned. Who let you down? What happened that made you feel like you are the only one that will be there for you? Your earliest memory of when you felt abandoned is the root cause of your clutter. Make peace with this memory. Accept what happened. Release it.

Once you make peace with the memory, begin to focus on where and how your life was abundant. Recall some ways in which you have been taken care of. From this awareness of the abundance in your life, think about what you want to make room for in your life. What do you really want? Now, hold the vision of what you want in your head as you make your way through the physical clutter in your space.

You are practicing radical self-love when you clear out clutter because you are making room for what you truly want and trusting that what you need will always be provided to you.

I release what I do not currently need with love and joy, knowing that what I need is available to me exactly when I need it.

77. YOU ALWAYS HAVE A CHOICE

So often, we get caught up in feeling like a victim – as if things are happening *to* us. Being a victim is a state of mind. Despite what happens to you, you can choose to have an empowered stance. Yes, even when something terrible happens to you.

In order to exercise a choice, you must first be mindful that you have a choice. No, you can't always choose the circumstances that happen to you. But, you can always choose how you respond to the situation. You can always choose to view each obstacle as an opportunity to grow and learn. You can realize that obstacles are presented to help you burst your limiting notions about who you are and what you can handle.

Think about a recent situation in your life that is upsetting. Perhaps it's an argument you've had with a loved one. Or maybe something happened around your job. What are you telling yourself about the situation or the person(s) involved that upsets you? What is the higher purpose for this situation? What are you meant to learn? With this knowledge, what will you choose to make this experience less upsetting?

You are practicing radical self-love when you realize that you always have the ability to choose your perspective on a situation and how you respond to it.

I make choices that empower me and cause me to grow and expand beyond my imagination.

78. Create a New Rule

Sometimes, we operate by default rules. When you operate by default rules, chances are you may have a few results that you don't like.

For example, let's say you always rush to return the call of a friend in crisis, but you are slow to return the call of a friend who is just calling to say "Hi." Recently, you notice that you don't have any friends who are able and willing to support you when *you* need a shoulder to lean on. What you may not realize is that you had a default rule which helped create the circumstance that you are currently in.

It's time to create a new rule. Is there a pattern that recurs in your life that you don't like? Perhaps you keep attracting the wrong partner or friends. Maybe you keep gaining weight. Once you are clear about the pattern, start investigating what your default rule is.

To determine your default rule, spend some time looking at your own behaviors. How do you show up? What actions are you taking (or not taking) that may be creating the results that you don't like?

Once you've determined your default rule, you can begin to consciously create a new rule. Start by thinking about the kinds of results you want. What would you need to do differently to create these results? How could you do these things consistently? By answering these questions, you begin to create new rules that attract what you truly want rather than what you've been getting.

You are practicing radical self-love when you cease living by default rules and live by rules you consciously create.

I am aware of my behaviors and default rules. I consciously choose to engage in behaviors, actions, and habits that give me the life I want.

79. Learn From Your Mistakes

We all make mistakes. Mistakes are an inevitable part of life. They provide us with an opportunity to grow and learn. The real tragedy is not in making mistakes, but in failing to learn from the mistakes you do make.

Once you finish lamenting about the mistake you made, take some time to objectively look at the situation. There is always something to learn. If you choose not to learn it now, the Universe will surely repeat the circumstances (usually in a harsher or more forceful way!) until you've learned what you are supposed to learn. You might as well spare a worse pain than what you're currently feeling by taking the time to learn your lessons now.

Here are a few questions you can ask yourself to help you learn from the experience:

- What did I do to contribute to the situation?
- What did the other person do to contribute to the situation?
- Where did I dishonor my values?
- How did this experience make me stronger or better?
- Is this a recurring pattern in my life?

After you evaluate your answers, ask yourself, "What do I get to do differently next time?" In doing so, you outline a game plan to help ensure that you learn your lesson and gain the fruits of your mistakes.

You are practicing radical self-love when you carve out the time to carefully evaluate and learn from your mistakes.

I accept mistakes are a natural part of life and I choose to learn from them, forgiving myself and releasing any negative feelings I carry.

80. Ask for Help

You don't need to be superwoman. You don't need to do it all by yourself. You may think that you can do it better, faster, or smarter than someone else. Regardless of your perception, ask for help.

You were never meant to do this alone. If you take some time to reflect, you'll recognize that you did not do this alone. Whose shoulders were you carried on? How were you taught to do the things that you do? With nearly everything you know, someone has helped you.

When people failed us, the Divine was always there – whispering to us about what we should do and what we should steer away from. Yet despite a history of being helped, we reach a place where we become resistant to asking for help.

Yes, you may appear vulnerable if you ask for help. So what? No, really. So what? That vulnerability could be the key to a deeper, richer relationship. It could make you prosperous. It could also make you lighter and free.

Change your expectation. Instead of expecting that people will fail you or somehow mishandle your vulnerability, expect that people are willing to help and are capable. They want to give. They want to support. After all, what you focus your attention on will manifest. You can choose to focus on how people will hurt or disappoint you, or you can choose to focus on what's possible with their support. Either way, the choice is yours.

You are practicing radical self-love when you let go of your ego and ask for help.

I free myself and circulate abundance by asking for help and receiving it.

81. Get Clear on Your Vision

When you have a vision of what you want, you are more likely to achieve it. Take some time to reflect on what's important to you and what you want. Identify your values. Spend some time really dreaming about what you want out of life. What is important to you in relationships? What does connection mean to you? Be very specific in defining the world that you want to create.

One way to capture your vision is through a vision board. A vision board is a visual representation of the life that you want. Make it a sacred experience. Begin by placing a symbol of spiritual significance at the top of your paper. Then look for images and words in magazines or on the internet that capture how you will *feel* when the life you dream of manifests. For example, if you want a baby, pick an image of an infant that really makes you feel your maternal instincts. Once you feel as if all of your vision is included, then write at the bottom of the vision board, "This or something better."

The key to a vision board is not just in its creation. In order to manifest it, you must contemplate your vision. Keep it at the forefront of your mind each day. Don't worry about whether you've captured everything. A vision board is organic – you can always add or create new ones as you evolve.

You are practicing radical self-love when you get clear on what you want for yourself. When you develop a vision for your life and consciously and consistently connect with that vision, you are helping to make that vision come to fruition.

I am clear about what I want and I take time each day to cultivate and manifest my vision.

82. Fake It 'Til You Make It

Henry David Thoreau wrote, "If one advances confidently in the direction of one's dreams, *and endeavors to live the life which one has imagined*, one will meet with a success unexpected in common hours." (emphasis added). Notice Thoreau did not say "dare to get there." He distinctly instructs us to *live* the life that we imagine.

When you live the life you imagine, you are sending a clear message to the Universe that not only is this the life that you want and expect, but that you can handle it. You are ready for that life. If you are having trouble living that life, ask yourself: "If I believed that this life was truly possible, what would I do? How would I act?" These questions help release you from your old paradigm, which keeps you stuck in your old habits, way of thinking, and circumstances. These questions are perfect for the doubting mind because they don't require your mind to believe that you have the life that you are longing for. It simply asks you to consider what you would do *if* it were true.

Sometimes, we have to fake it 'til we make it. It's the only way to help our minds readjust to a higher frequency. And that higher frequency is essential for us to actually manifest what we truly desire.

You are practicing radical self-love when you dare to live as if you already have the life that you want and are the person you want to become. Experiment. Start asking yourself the questions that will put you in the frame of mind of the woman you wish to become.

I know what I want. I take the next step confidently in the direction of my dreams, knowing that what I cultivate on the inside manifests on the outside, and living as if I already have it.

83. You Reap What You Sow; Choose Your Seeds Wisely

There are two levels to your mind: the conscious mind and your subconscious mind. You have a gift – you can choose what you plant in you conscious mind. With your awareness, you are able to decide what thoughts you will think, what types of movies you will watch, what types of books you will read, and what type of people you will associate with. All of these choices have an impact on your conscious mind.

But, this gift is even greater than you realize. With persistence, your conscious mind can reprogram your subconscious mind. Let's assume you feel like an outsider. You have played this record for so long that your subconscious creates and recreates experiences that affirm this notion that you don't belong. You could begin a consistent regimen to change your conscious thoughts. At first, you won't believe the affirmations. That's why we say, "Fake it 'til you make it." But, continue to work at it anyway. Over time, you will start to notice that there are a few places where you feel like you do belong. Then you'll notice it happen more and more. Each time you see the new conscious thought manifest, you can be assured that you are successfully reprogramming your subconscious mind.

You are practicing radical self-love when you consciously direct your thoughts to focus on what you want, thereby reprogramming your subconscious mind, which, in turn, will manifest these new thoughts.

I reap a life of abundance and joy because I sow positive thoughts in the fertile soil of my mind.

84. Stop Rendering Yourself Invisible

Do you feel invisible sometimes? Like no one cares about what you care about or what you want? If so, there may be a part of you that believes you do not have a right to take up space – as if you don't matter.

What happens in our external world is a manifestation of what is happening on the inside. You may not consciously believe it, but there is a part of you that feels that it is best to keep yourself in the closet. There is a reason why you attract situations where you feel invisible. You have to get to the root cause.

To discover the root cause, ask yourself, "How is my invisibility serving me?" Does it protect you from having to put yourself out there? Does it mean that you don't have to step up and do something that scares you? Does it allow you to stay in your comfort zone? Would you feel too vulnerable?

Once you discover the root cause, you get to make a choice. Think about what you gain from the invisibility versus what it costs you. How do you really want to show up? If the costs of being invisible outweigh the benefits, then it is time to make a change. Change your internal dialogue so that you will not be invisible anymore. Know that you can handle any challenge visibility creates. If you don't already have the tools, they will be given to you. You just have to make a conscious decision and trust that you will be given what you need to make your visibility a safe and successful experience.

You are practicing radical self-love when you take the steps necessary to clear out the beliefs within you that render you invisible.

I am worthy of making my presence, thoughts, and ideas known.

85. Savor your Successes, Your Almost Successes & Your "I-Completely-Blew-It" Moments

Life is a gift, but it is short. And the older you get, the faster it seems to go. So, it's important to really enjoy and savor your life. *All* of it.

Savor your successes. How many times have you set goals for yourself, reached them (or got really close to reaching them), and before you could celebrate, you're already focused on the next thing. You never bother to celebrate the victory. Stop this cycle. It deprives you of the ability to value yourself and your accomplishments. More importantly, it prevents you from having a moment to reflect with gratitude.

Savor your near successes. Rather than focusing on what you didn't accomplish, focus on what you did. You've come a long way! And it's worth relishing that.

Savor your "I-completely-blew-it!" moments. Even though you may have made a mistake or didn't accomplish what you set out to do, there is a wonderful lesson to learn. These opportunities show us what we need to develop and where we can grow. Moreover, this gives you an opportunity to learn to love yourself even in the face of your mistakes or so-called failures. The opportunity will only be a failure if you choose not to learn from it.

You are practicing radical self-love when you celebrate all of the facets of your life. Each moment – good and bad – presents an opportunity to love yourself more deeply.

My life is an adventure and I celebrate the ups, downs and in-between's of my life!

86. ACCEPT YOUR MIND

Radical self-love requires you to accept your mind. Your mind is both the holder of infinite possibility and infinite doubt. The same mind that can visualize a goal is the same mind that can derail that goal by producing a fear-based thought.

Mental self-acceptance requires you to become aware of the full spectrum of your mind. Once you are aware, you can cultivate a healthier mind by choosing healthier thoughts and eliminating negative ones.

Our thinking is unhealthy when we engage in what Dr. David Burns calls "distorted thinking" in his book *Feeling Good*. We engage in distorted thinking by:

(1) engaging in all-or-nothing thinking;
(2) viewing a negative event as a never-ending pattern;
(3) dwelling on the negatives and ignoring the positives;
(4) discrediting positive qualities and accomplishments;
(5) concluding that things are bad without definitive evidence;
(6) magnifying or minimizing the importance of things;
(7) reasoning from feelings rather than from logic;
(8) criticizing oneself or others with "should" statements;
(9) labeling oneself ("I'm a loser"); and
(10) blaming oneself or another.

Which of these patterns do you engage in?

You are practicing radical self-love when you recognize the ways in which you distort your thinking and develop healthier ways to use your mind.

I redirect my distorted thinking patterns and choose to use my mind for the creation of a life of infinite possibilities and abundance.

87. YOUR CIRCUMSTANCES DO NOT DICTATE YOUR OUTCOME

Things happen in your life. They are the facts of your life. But, they do not determine the outcome of your life. You choose whether you allow the facts of your life to have power over you.

Let's say you were cheated on by a former partner. The fact is that you were betrayed. But, you still get to choose how you will allow that to affect your life. Will you choose to never be in an intimate relationship again because you are afraid of being hurt? Will you make fake attempts at love by pretending to be willing to be in a relationship, but always looking for what's wrong or a way out? Or will you choose to accept what happened, becoming aware of what you believed or did that may have welcomed such an experience and allowing yourself to love again? In all three instances, the facts did not change; only the power you gave those facts changed.

Take a moment to think about something in your life where you may be allowing the facts to dictate the results. Notice what power you gave to the circumstance. What result do you really want? What would it take for you to get there? What beliefs about yourself, another, or the circumstance do you need to change in order to get the result that you truly want?

You are practicing radical self-love when you accept the facts for what they are, but refuse to let them dictate your results.

I always have a choice about how I view the facts of my life and what power I give them. At any given moment, I can change the relationship I have with my past.

88. Abolish the Lie

To have radical self-love you must abolish the lies. You are not bad. You are not unworthy. You are not less than or greater than anyone or anything else. You are one with God. You are one with nature. You are one with all living things. We all share the same pulse.

Your fingers look very different than your belly, but it is all you. So, too, do the different aspects of God look different, but that doesn't change the fact that they are all a part of God.

Wake up from the nightmare you have created by believing the lies. Know that you can uncreate the nightmare. It will take some work because you have been trained to think of yourself as something much smaller and much less significant than what you truly are. But none of that is true.

When you dare to abolish the lies, fear and resistance will come up. You will experience setbacks. Don't fear the setbacks. They are created by our limited self (our ego, our mind), which is desperately trying to stay in control.

When the setbacks show up, give it space. Observe it. Listen to it. But notice that you are separate from it. There is a greater part of you that has the capacity to observe what is going on.

You are practicing radical self-love when you choose to abolish all lies that suggest that you are less than all that you truly are.

I accept my truth that I am one with God. I am worthy, loved, loving, good, joyous, powerful, and valuable. No thoughts that contradict this truth may take residence in my mind.

89. Trick Your Paradigm

You have been given an incredible gift – your mind. But this is not a gift that takes care of itself. You must train it. You must notice what it is thinking. If you don't pay attention to it, it will get out of hand.

Your mind has been programmed with messages from your family, your environment, and the media. Unfortunately, most of our society operates from a paradigm of limited consciousness. This paradigm operates from a place of scarcity, lack, and fear. As a result, most people think from a place of what they *can* do as opposed to what they would *love* to do.

You have been taught very well how to follow the paradigm. Haven't you ever had someone say to you "Don't be ridiculous? That's impossible." And most of the time, when others created the doubt in your mind, your brilliant ideas began to dim – sometimes you let it go completely out.

If you want to break the cycle of living a life based on perceived limitations rather than perceived possibilities, then you have to trick your paradigm. Whenever you doubt that you can really do something that your heart desires, ask yourself this one question: "If I believed that it were possible, what would I do?" Then act from that place. By asking this question, you are creating doubt about your doubt!

You are practicing radical self-love when you trick your old paradigm of limited thinking into believing that what you dare to dream is possible.

I can achieve anything that I think of. I choose to see what is possible and I invite Spirit to show me the way to achieve my dreams.

90. Stop Shoulding All Over Yourself

There are two types of shoulds: (1) shoulds based on messages from others; and (2) shoulds that come from within. Shoulds based on messages from others are when you internalize the opinions and standards of your family, friends, or society at large. If these messages resonate with you, it will not be a should. It will just be.

However, when it doesn't resonate, you will have resistance. You will feel torn and confused. You think, "I should do that, but I don't really want to. I don't know what to do!"

Shoulds that come from within are generally related to self-care. It's the voice within that nudges you to go to the gym, eat healthy, and take a vacation. Although these shoulds are intended for self-care, the mere presence of the "should" indicates self-judgment and resistance. Take the time to explore your resistance. It will give you an opportunity to see what you are truly longing for. Maybe, you don't feel like going to the gym because you'd rather walk outside. Or maybe you want to keep eating the cake or potato chips because you're longing for comfort. By exploring the resistance to the "self-care shoulds," you can find a healthier, life-affirming way to satisfy your underlying needs.

You are practicing radical self-love when you stop shoulding all over yourself. The presence of a should indicates some form of internal resistance – either because the messages don't resonate or because you are longing for something different. Be loving and compassionate with yourself and allow yourself to have what you truly want.

I honor and respect my true needs and wants.

91. The Presence of Your Saboteur Means That You are on to Something Really Big

The Saboteur is the part of you that sabotages your efforts. When you find your Saboteur acting up and kicking up a fuss, chances are, you are really on to something *BIG!* Something that your heart truly desires.

The more you step into your possibilities and your heart's desires, the louder and more persistent your Saboteur will get. Your Saboteur is rooted in the primitive part of your brain -- the stem of your brain, which houses your instinctual "fight-or-flight" reaction. Our ancestors were able to survive, in part, by sticking with what was familiar. As a result, we have a pre-programmed part of us that compels us to stick with the familiar to stay safe. Your Saboteur is fighting to keep you in what is familiar – even if it isn't working for you – because it thinks it's safe to do so.

When you notice the resistance coming up, recognize that it is your Saboteur trying to protect you. But, you know better than that. You know that if you stick with only what is familiar, you miss out on all the rest that is possible. You miss out on an opportunity to grow. So, instead of beating yourself up for having the Saboteur show up and foil your plans, allow yourself to remember that it just means that you are on to something *big!*

You are practicing radical self-love when you observe your Saboteur without going into judgment of yourself for having self-sabotaging thoughts.

I now know that the presence of the Saboteur simply means that I am on to something BIG. I am growing and evolving, stretching the boundaries of who I was into more fully experiencing the infinite being that I am!

92. Make Your Future Self Your New Best Friend

You're future self is where it's at! Take a minute to connect with her. Take a deep breath. In your mind's eye imagine that you could see your future self. She is the best version of you that you can imagine. Really take her in. What does she look like? Where does she live? What do you notice about her energy? What is she doing with her time? How does she generate income? What makes her happy? Get to know her. Isn't she magnificent? Can't you feel her radiance?

What you envisioned is absolutely possible. If it weren't, you wouldn't have been able to create it in your mind. Everything is created twice. First, in thought. Second, through manifestation of the thought in physical form. Think about it; the shirt you're wearing was first a thought in someone's mind before it was physically created. So, likewise, the fact that you can envision your future self is the first creation of her. Now, you just need to make more of her manifest in the physical form.

To manifest your future self, make her your best friend. Let her guide you. Mimic her. What would she do if she were in your situation? When you cultivate a stronger intimate relationship with your future self, you will become her more quickly. Give yourself permission to manifest the very best version of you.

You are practicing radical self-love when you allow your future self to become your best friend and confidant. Get to know her. Trust her. She will never let you down!

I embrace and step into my future self. She is me and I am her NOW!

93. YOU ARE ENOUGH

You are enough. In fact, you are more than enough – you are abundant. Maybe you forgot that you are enough. Perhaps you thought that you are damaged goods. Has someone in your past hurt you, leaving you feeling lost, abandoned and like you were less than? Or did you receive messages that kept insisting that who you are was not enough?

We live in a society that thrives on comparisons and competition. There are the haves and the have nots. There are the straight A students and the C students. There are the rich and the poor.

When we compare ourselves to others, we demean ourselves and the other person – regardless of whether the comparison makes you temporarily feel better about yourself. Comparing ourselves to another tends to make us cling to our separateness from one another. When you feel better than someone, then you are bound to feel worse about yourself in the presence of another person that you perceive as better than you.

The key is to recognize that you are enough – just as you are. The skills, talents, and gifts you have are enough. They are perfectly suited so you can do what you are put on this Earth to do. You have a mission and you have been given absolutely everything – including the challenging times – to ensure that you execute your mission perfectly.

You are practicing radical self-love when you stop comparing yourself to others and realize that who you are and what you have is more than enough.

I am more than enough and I have all that I need to fulfill my divine purpose.

94. Never Excuse Yourself

You are on the path toward radical self-love. There is no room for excuses here. Excuses seek to relieve you of your obligations to yourself. Excuses take up valuable energy and don't serve you in the long-run. They keep you small because they keep you in the same paradigm that you have been in.

We make excuses for our behavior all the time. We'll come up with justifications for why we break the commitments we make to ourselves, like exercising, leaving work at a decent hour, or taking a spa day. Each time you break a commitment to yourself, you are mitigating how much you can trust yourself.

You are in a relationship with yourself. It must be cultivated. Just like you can feel abandoned or distrust in a relationship with another, so too, can you feel that with yourself.

When you notice that you are making excuses for your own behaviors, stop. Ask yourself, "If I accepted full responsibility for my actions, what would I do?" What would help you move into a place of integrity with yourself? Do you need to renegotiate your agreement with yourself? Do you need to recommit to your action items? Do you need to break your actions into smaller steps? Do whatever it takes to put yourself back in integrity with yourself.

You are practicing radical self-love when you refuse to excuse yourself and choose to accept full responsibility for your life.

I keep the promises I make to myself. I mean what I say and I say what I mean. I accept full responsibility for my actions and I make adjustments when necessary.

95. Don't Forsake the Long-term Goals for Short-term Satisfaction

According to Buddhist philosophy, a person is considered wise when they are able to forgo short-term gain for the sake of their long-term goal. How important it is for all of us to adopt this philosophy! Especially in this era of instant gratification.

In the short-term, many things can appear to be appealing, even when their long term effects are harmful. In the short-term, it is convenient to drink out of plastic bottles, but in the long-term, it harms our Earth. In the short-term, it may be appealing to experience the thrill of an affair, but in the long-term, it can devastate your relationship. In the short-term, it may feel good to buy yourself some things that you can't really afford, but in the long-term, you could ruin your credit and future buying power (not to mention your peace of mind when bill collectors come calling!).

When you make decisions based on short-term gain at the sake of achieving your long-term goals, you are short-changing yourself.

You are practicing radical self-love when you generally choose to favor your long-term goals over short-term satisfaction. Acting to the contrary only serves to sabotage the life that you truly want. If you think about it, you'll realize that there wasn't any real happiness in the short-term satisfaction any way. It was merely a distraction and a delusion!

I am more powerful than the short-term temptations that surround me and threaten to derail me from my goals. I love and value myself enough to know that I will have lasting happiness when I put my long-term goals before short-term desires.

96. Support vs. Help

Although both "help" and "support" are ways of assisting a person, there is a difference between them. Support means doing something that contributes to someone's capacity. Help means doing something for another person so that they need not do it themselves. Over time, support will help increase the development, skill and creativity of the supported person. It will ultimately level the playing field. Help, on the other hand, will tend to create dependency between the provider and the recipient. If prolonged, the recipient may feel incapable.

Neither support nor help are inherently bad or good. The key is to know what you want. If you are the person seeking assistance, think about whether you are in a real jam and you just want someone to help you get out of it. If you do, then you'll want help. If, instead, you want to grow and develop, then you'll want support.

If you are the person providing assistance, then you need to be clear about what the other person wants and what is in the best interest of the relationship.

Too often, we women tend to provide help and it leaves us feeling drained and exhausted because we're constantly doing for other people. If that's the case, think about how you can change the dynamics so that the other person can acquire more responsibility. Sure, it may take them a bit longer at first, but in the long run, it will benefit the both of you.

You are practicing radical self-love when you consciously consider whether you want to provide or receive help or support. In general, strive to provide and receive support.

I consciously choose assistance that is for the highest good of all.

97. A Small Grain of Fear May be Blocking Your Success

Have you ever wanted something so badly, but you just can't seem to get it despite your best efforts? Maybe you want to get pregnant, meet the perfect mate, or make more money. You keep taking action, but you're just not getting there. Well, you may have a grain of fear looming in the background.

Believe it or not, a mere grain of fear can block your blessings. Fear is a powerful emotion, and even the slightest presence of it can prevent you from having what you truly want. Fear can paralyze you. It can prevent you from taking actions that would lead you in the direction of your dreams.

If you're not seeing the results you want, get quiet and check in. Ask the Diving to reveal whether you have some hidden fears. Are you afraid you're not worthy? Are you afraid of the responsibility that you will have to assume if you get what you want? Do you inadvertently believe that what you long for, if accomplished, will conflict with some of your other values? For example, you may think, "If I get this opportunity, I won't be able to spend time with my loved ones." Once you discover the underlying fear, you can take the necessary steps to overcome it. The first step is to notice that it's there.

You are practicing radical self-love when you realize that the presence of a mere grain of fear can block your blessings. It's as if a small voice inside of you whispers to the Universe, "Cancel that order!"

I welcome the truth. I invite the Divine to show me clearly and vividly any fears and contradictions that I hold that prevent me from accomplishing my dreams so that I may release them.

98. Overcome Your Fears

Everyone has fears. Sometimes they serve a rational purpose, such as protecting you from a life-threatening situation. Many fears, however, are irrational and prevent you from taking necessary action to achieving what you truly want. Most people want to overcome their fears, but aren't sure how. Here are four steps that you can immediately implement to help overcome your fears.

1. ***Identify the Fear.*** There are many types of fear - fear of success, fear of failure, fear of being judged, fear of death, fear of commitment, etc. Identify your specific fear. Using a scale of 1-10, how intense is your fear?
2. ***Discover the Underlying Limiting Belief.*** Underneath each fear is a limiting belief that fuels the fear. For example, a person may fear success because they believe that it would compromise time with family.
3. ***Challenge the Limiting Belief.*** For each limiting belief, ask yourself the following question: "What's *not* true about this belief?" Get creative in finding evidence that contradicts the belief.
4. ***Visualize Conquering the Fear.*** Get a vivid picture of yourself conquering the fear and its underlying belief. Notice how different you feel without the fear and limiting belief. While staying in the visualization, ask yourself, "What did I do to get here?" Commit to doing these things.

You are practicing radical self-love when you commit to taking the foregoing steps to overcome your fears.

I am fearless. I walk confidently in the direction of my dreams.

99. Stuck? Try a Different Perspective

When you feel stuck, you are thinking about the situation in a way that prevents you from seeing another possible solution. The key to getting unstuck is to change your perspective or point of view.

You can shift the way you think about a situation by being open to embracing another way of looking at it. Don't take yourself too seriously and allow yourself to experiment. Now, we can begin playing!

Draw a big circle on a piece of paper, and divide it into 4 slices. Think of a situation where you are stuck. Place the name of the situation at the top of the page. Make sure that the name is neutral and does not express a particular viewpoint. For example, if you are stuck around whether to quit a job, name the situation "Career".

Give each slice of the pie a name. Get creative here. Think of different people, places and things that intrigue you, and use that as the basis to name each slice. Identify some qualities or characteristics about the person or thing that you've named. Now, for each slice ask yourself, "How would the situation look from this angle?" For example, let's say you wrote "tree" in one of your slices, which represents rooted majesty to you. What would the situation look like if you felt rooted and majestic about the situation? What kinds of solutions are possible from that perspective?

Once you have tried on the situation from each perspective, choose the one that feels the best. Now take action only from that perspective!

You are practicing radical self-love when you choose the perspective from which you operate.

I open my heart and mind to new ways of thinking and new possibilities!

100. Make Peace with Your Mental Monster

All of us seek to enjoy the abundance of life, yet sometimes, there is a gnawing voice in the back of our minds that prevents us from receiving and appreciating the full abundance life has to offer. This is your "mental monster" and it serves as a barrier to your overall happiness.

A mental monster is the monster in your head that scares you into inaction based on its negative comments. It says things like, "Who do you think you are? You're not good enough, smart enough, attractive enough, etc." Sound familiar? Many of us have more than one of these monsters claiming residence in our minds. Have no fear; here are some tips to make peace with your monster:

- *Notice when it is talking.* When the thoughts are negative, limiting, or self-sabotaging, it's usually a mental monster speaking. Listen deeply as the voice of some monsters are faint (but harmful nonetheless). Simply bringing them to light can release them from you.
- *Have your mental monster draw a self-portrait.* Whenever you feel powerless by the negative thoughts in your head, pull out the picture. Realize that the negative thoughts may be in you, but they are not of you. Use the picture as a reminder that you are separate from the negative thoughts.
- *Get up and Move!* Mental monsters tend to multiply and fester when you are stagnant. They rarely chatter while we are engaged in a physical activity. So, next time you feel a monster attack, get up and move your body–exercise, dance, stomp your feet or take a brisk

walk. Just do something that will shake up the energy source that is feeding your mental monster.

- ***Invoke Your Ideal Self.*** Whenever you can't make a decision because of a mental monster, stop and bring an image of your ideal self to mind. Then ask her, "What should I do?" Follow the path of your ideal self.

You are practicing radical self-love when you consistently and repeatedly use these tools to help you make peace with your mental monster so that you can make room for the things that you really want.

I choose to live my best possible life. The mental monsters in my mind are no match for me! I am powerful, loved, and more than enough!

101. CHOOSE HAPPINESS NOW

Happiness is not out there. It does not need a partner, job, children, or pets to exist. Happiness is within you. It is your natural state. Your divine essence is a happy one. Yet, you may have forgotten this. No need to worry – most of us have.

We live in a world that makes unhappiness, lack and strife the norm. But in this instance, what is "normal" is not actually natural. You are a joy-filled being who is here to have an ever-expanded version of life and joy.

Choose to reconnect with your natural state. Choose happiness.

How can you choose happiness when everything is falling apart? Simple. Because even when things fall apart, there is something to be happy about. In the midst of death and dying, be happy about the love and compassion that you see and feel. At the end of a relationship, be happy about what you have learned, how you have grown, and how you are now releasing what doesn't fit you for a relationship that will. During poor physical health, be happy about the parts of your body that are working and healthy. Pay them mind.

You are practicing radical self-love each time you choose happiness. Happiness is always available to you.

There is so much for me to be joyful about and I am happy!

ABOUT THE AUTHOR

You know how some women are so unhappy with themselves and their lives that no matter how hard they try to fix things, they just can't seem to shake that deep hollow emptiness inside? They aren't happy with their weight, job, relationships, and most of all themselves. Regardless of all that they've accomplished, they're constantly beating themselves up. They want to be happy and know that life's got to be better than this, but just don't know how to do it.

Ann Thomas, Esq., CPCC, is a certified life coach who helps women who are tired of feeling unhappy stop the endless cycle of stinkin' thinkin' and the self-sabotaging antics that follow. Ann helps women find true, lasting, nothing-can-take-it-from-you happiness. She does this by teaching radical self-love -- empowering women to connect with their divinity and love and accept themselves unconditionally. The motto of Ann's company, Evolving Goddess, says it all: "Fall in love with yourself and your life <u>will</u> fall into place!"

The reason Ann is so committed to helping women get out of their own personal hell is because she was there. Ann knew first-hand the devastating impact lack of self-love and self-acceptance can have. As a result of persevering through over sixteen years of despair, she found a way to live a happy and empowered life. Today, she lives a life she loves and uses her experiences to help other women do the same in a loving and compassionate, yet no-nonsense, way.

Begin your journey to radical self-love by reading this book.

WANT SOME EXTRA SUPPORT IN YOUR JOURNEY TOWARD RADICAL SELF-LOVE?

I'm here to support you in your journey to unconditionally love and accept yourself so that you can finally live the life that you've always dreamed of. **As my gift to you for reading this book, I'd like to offer you a FREE 30 minute coaching call.** Take advantage of this amazing absolutely free offer. Call or email me at the address below. I look forward to hearing from you. Remember, when you fall in love with yourself, your life <u>will</u> fall into place!

Evolving Goddess
www.EvolvingGoddess.com
Ann@EvolvingGoddess.com
(641) 715-3900, Ext. 74522

Visit our website www.EvolvingGoddess.com and grab your FREE copy of my special report – *Surviving the Dip: 10 Steps to Bounce Back Better Than Ever After Rejection*. This report is your chance to be on the fast-track to happiness. **The support is here. It's your choice to take advantage of it!**

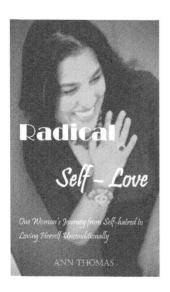

COMING SPRING 2012 . . .

Radical Self-Love: *One Woman's Journey from Self-hatred to Loving Herself Unconditionally.*

In this heart-warming, yet provocative book, get an intimate look at the author's personal and spiritual journey toward unconditional self-love. Available at select stores, Amazon, and www.EvolvingGoddess.com.